# San Juan Islands Travel Guide

## A Land and Sea Guidebook
## For all Travelers

**Turn Point Lighthouse and Museum**

Copyright © 2017 John Cummins
All rights reserved. Individuals may copy and reproduce pages for personal use.

# WHAT'S INSIDE THIS GUIDEBOOK

State Parks
    County Parks
        City Parks
            DNR Parks - Dept. Of Natural Resources
                Marine Parks
                    Cascadia Marine Trail Campsites
                Dog Parks
Cities
    Villages
        Resorts
            Marinas
                Campgrounds
Day hikes
    Kayak launch sites
        Boat ramps and long term parking
            Bicycling trips, boating itineraries, kayaking trips
                How to use the free inter-island ferries to create great outings
                Transit stops and ferry travel made easy
Marine fuel stops
    Grocery stores
        Island back doors - local knowledge - public beach access
        Maps - charts - honest helpful reviews

**"This travelers guidebook has one primary purpose"**

That purpose is - cut through the hype - tell it like it is - include what is needed.

As skipper or chief travel planner, use this guide as a resource to help you plan before leaving home. Take it with you to save time, frustration, money, and headache.

The best trips, travels, and vacations are the ones that you dream of before you go – and then relive after you return. They are fun filled, sometimes action packed, enjoyable outings that you talk about later and look forward to continuing.

Think of this guide as your best friend in the islands.

# San Juan Islands Travel Guide
*"Land and Sea Guidebook"*

This travel guidebook is for all visitors to the San Juan Islands, and very importantly, it includes advice and tips about key cities, parks, marinas and resort facilities needed to make your visit a success. Cars, boats, kayaks, and bicycles are the preferred mode of travel, sometimes all on the same day. The inter-island ferry system is free to foot passengers and cyclists. How to put it to use is in the book.

In the interest of not publishing dated, obsolete, useless information, I have taken care not to include overly fluff filled articles and reviews.

My comments and hints are from firsthand experience, I have personally traveled, boated, and yes, bicycled all the islands, villages, parks and communities.

I don't sugar-coat anything, but I do rave, and where appropriate, I rant a little. My focus is bringing you important facts, budget minded useful suggestions, and time tested tips for traveling this vacation wonderland called the San Juans.

This is my second travel guide to the San Juans. The original published in 2014, *"San Juan Islands Cruise Guide,"* is still your detailed boaters bible to the marine parks. The new guide is titled "San Juan Islands Travel Guide." It includes shore attractions, e.g. resorts, campgrounds, villages, parks, and lots of local community knowledge chosen to assist your sightseeing.

*This guide is a companion resource to the cruise guide - not a replacement. Boat travelers to the San Juans should own and carry both.*

"San Juan Islands Travel Guide" + "San Juan Islands Cruise Guide"

Load your car and pack your bags,
bring your bikes, boats, kayaks, pets and children to the
San Juans today .

thanks - John

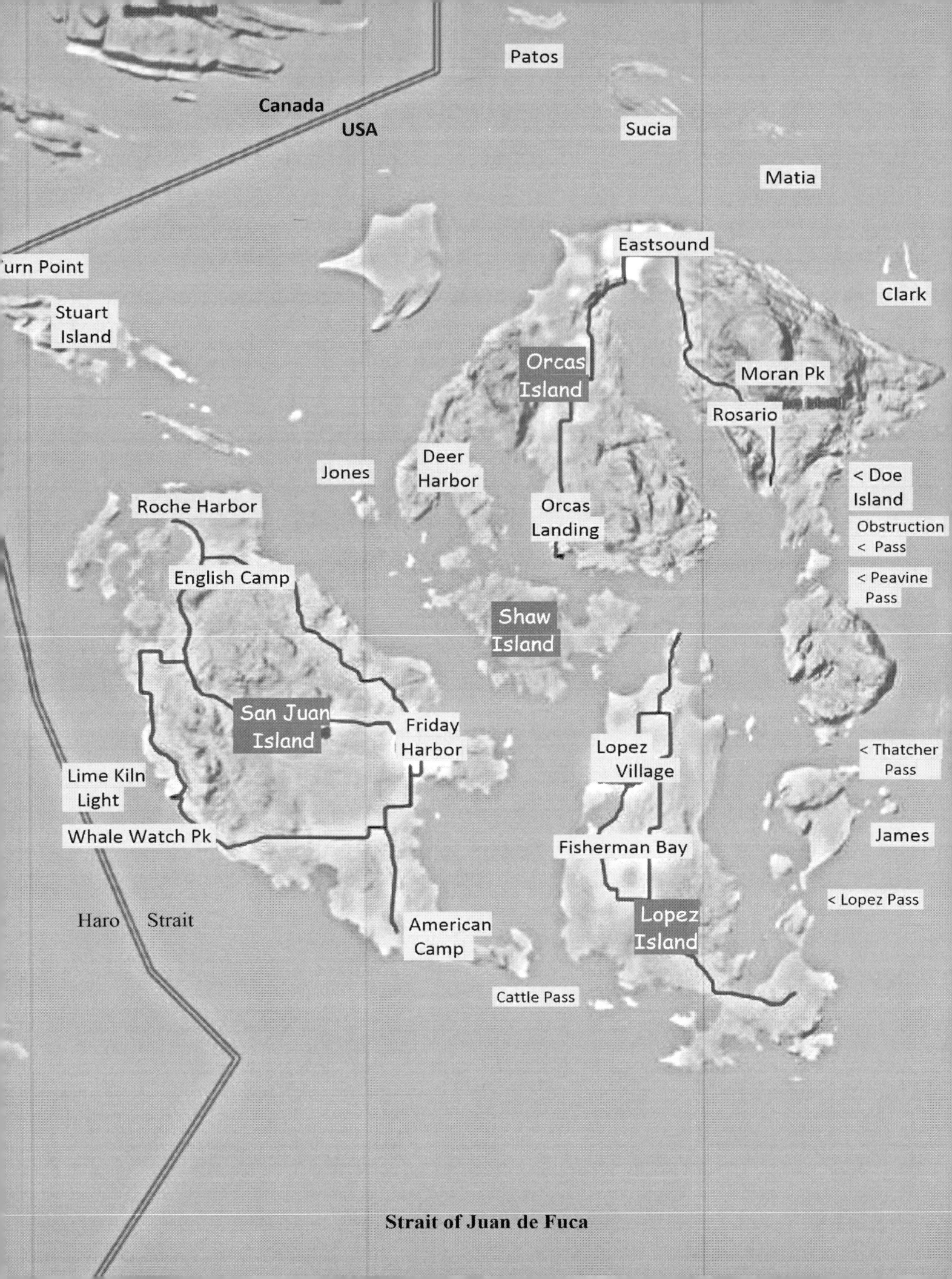

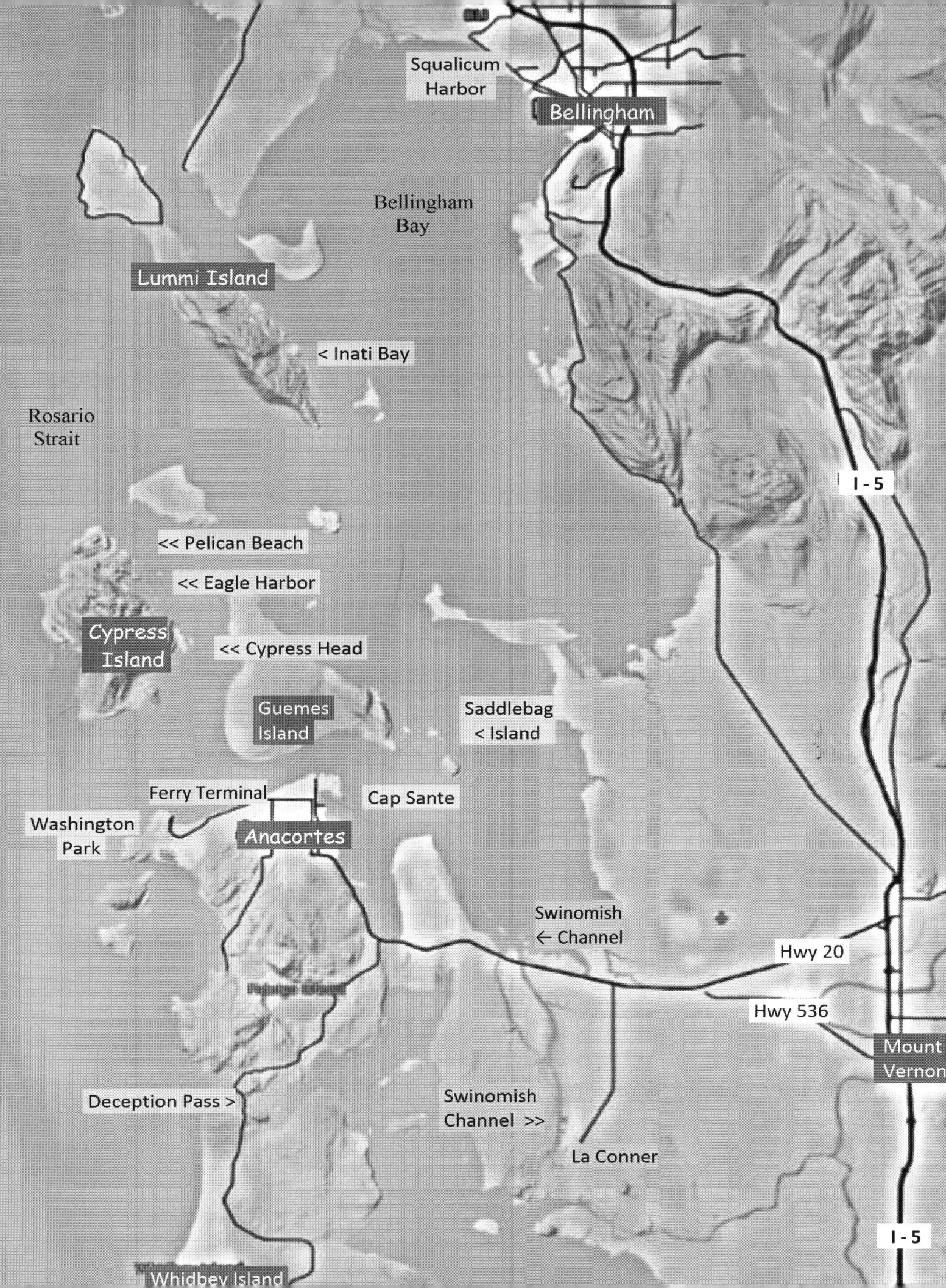

# Top Ten Destinations in the San Juans in Order of Importance

It is next to impossible to go anywhere worthwhile and see or do everything, which is likely how this next question stays with us. "If you only had one day and could only go to one place in the San Juans, where would it be?"

I answer that question resoundingly with, "Friday Harbor" - hands down, there is no other choice. However what if you have two or more days, and what if your interests are more sophisticated than average folk. The answer is still Friday Harbor, but I have listed 10 places in my opinion are the best choices for your consideration.

1. Friday Harbor (marina and town)
2. Lookout tower on top of Mt. Constitution
3. Deception Pass ( bridge hike)
4. Ride a ferry
5. Roche Harbor
6. Lime Kiln Point Park
7. Sculpture Park
8. Rosario (museum)
9. Whale Museum
10. Matia Island trail hike

## Bicycle Challenges

1. Ride from Orcas landing to the top of Mt constitution.
2. Ride the length of Lopez Island and back to ferry.
3. Circle San Juan Island, hitting Pear Point, Cattle Point, Whale Watch Park and Tarte Park.

## Hiking Challenges

1. Hike Turtleback Mtn.
2. Hike Mt Constitution.
3. Hike Young Hill.
4. Hike Eagle bluff. (My favorite)
5. Hike from Agate Beach to Iceberg Point.

## Kayaking Challenges

1. Circle Shaw Island.
2. Paddle to Jones, Sucia, Matia, James or Pelican Beach and camp.
3. Camp at SJ county park and paddle to Whale Watch Park
4. If you don't own a kayak – go on a guided tour.

## Subdued Challenges

1. Take the San Juan Transit "Sunset Tour to Lime Kiln Park.
2. Take a "Whale Watching" excursion boat tour.
3. Go on a "Windjammer Tall Ships" cruise.
4. Arrange to visit Friday Harbor or Roche Harbor for a 4th of July celebration.

There is lots more to do and see depending on your interests, but with these choices you can't go wrong. Nor can you complete all of them on one trip. (super challenge)

Our experience has been making multiple visits over the years, each time pushing our horizons and expanding our interests, but still visiting tried and true haunts and hideaways. Bringing along bicycles opened new dimensions to our travels. Bringing boats, dinghies and kayaks even more.

I recommend you not try do it all, just try to do it well, and when you wrap up a visit to go home, make a plan to come back. This system has worked well for us and judging by the familiar faces and acquaintances we cross paths with, it works well for others as well.

# Contents

WHAT'S INSIDE THIS GUIDEBOOK?........................................................................2
    Top Ten Destinations in the San Juans in Order of Importance.............................6
*WELCOME and proximity map*.............................................................................10
Using this Guidebook...............................................................................................11
About the San Juan's................................................................................................12
Gateway to the San Juans — Finding Anacortes....................................................14
    The Anacortes Ferry Terminal..............................................................................16
Bringing Your Boat to the San Juan's.......................................................................20
    Boat Ramps - Travel lifts......................................................................................21
San Juan Island - Friday Harbor..............................................................................23
    San Juan Island — Quick Check Map.................................................................24
    Friday Harbor Marina Map...................................................................................29
    Friday Harbor Downtown Area Map....................................................................30
    San Juan Island Transit Bus Stops......................................................................31
    RV Camping at the Fairgrounds in Friday Harbor...............................................32
    Turn Island State Park & Turn Point Day Use Area.............................................33
    Lafarge Open Space............................................................................................35
    Jackson Beach Park.............................................................................................36
    American Camp...................................................................................................37
    Eagle Cove Beach...............................................................................................39
    Pelindaba Lavender Farm....................................................................................40
    Krystal Acres Alpaca Farm and Country Store....................................................40
English Camp..........................................................................................................41
For Boaters - Garrison Bay and English Camp.......................................................43
English Camp - Roche Harbor Proximity Map.........................................................44
San Juan County Park at Smallpox Bay..................................................................45
    Smallpox Bay.......................................................................................................46
Lime Kiln Point Lighthouse and Whale Watch Park.................................................47
San Juan Islands Sculpture Park.............................................................................49
Afterglow Vista Mausoleum......................................................................................53
Roche Harbor Resort and Marina............................................................................55
    For Boaters Going to Roche Harbor...................................................................60
    Dinghy Docks at Roche Harbor...........................................................................62
    Roche Harbor Map...............................................................................................64
Lakedale Resort at Three Lakes..............................................................................65
Rueben Tarte Memorial Park...................................................................................66

Stuart Island..................................................................................................................67
    Prevost Harbor float..................................................................................69
    Reid Harbor float......................................................................................70
    Trail to Turn Point Lighthouse....................................................................70
    Boundary Pass Traders..............................................................................71
    Stuart Island County Dock..........................................................................73
Kayaking and small boats from Roche Harbor to Reid Harbor..................................73
Jones Island.................................................................................................74
Orcas Island Quick Check Map.........................................................................79
    Orcas Island Transit Stops..........................................................................80
    West Sound.............................................................................................81
    Turtleback Mountain.................................................................................82
    Deer Harbor............................................................................................83
    Eastsound................................................................................................84
    Eastsound Dog Park..................................................................................85
    Eastsound County Dock.............................................................................86
    West Beach Resort Marina.........................................................................87
    Rosario Resort.........................................................................................88
    For Boaters Going to Rosario.....................................................................90
    Cars and Bicyclists Headed to Rosario.........................................................90
    Moran State Park.....................................................................................91
    Olga........................................................................................................93
    Obstruction Pass State Park.......................................................................94
Doe Island State Park....................................................................................96
Clark Island State Park..................................................................................97
Matia Island State Park.................................................................................97
Sucia Island State Park..................................................................................98
    Echo Bay - Fossil Bay - Shallow Bay - Fox Cove - Ewing Cove - Snoring Cove........98
Patos Island Marine Park..............................................................................101
Inati Bay....................................................................................................102
Cypress Island............................................................................................103
    Pelican Beach - Eagle Harbor - Cypress Head..............................................103
Saddlebag Island State Marine Park...............................................................106
Swinomish Channel…………Map on pg 108..........................................................107
La Conner..................................................................................................107
Deception Pass State Park (marine park).........................................................109
    Cornet Bay - Bowman Bay - Sharpe Cove - Rosario Beach..............................109
Hope Island - Skagit Island - Goat Island - Fort Whitman....................................115

**Anacortes** ............................................................................................................. 117
    **Cap Sante Marina** ........................................................................................ 119
    **Washington Park** ......................................................................................... 120
**James Island Marine Park** ................................................................................... 121
**Blakely's** .............................................................................................................. 122
**Lopez Island** ........................................................................................................ 123
    **Lopez Island Quick Check Map** .................................................................. 124
    **Lopez Island Transit stops** ........................................................................... 125
    **Lopez Village** ............................................................................................... 126
    **For Boaters and Kayakers** ........................................................................... 127
    **Odlin County Park** ....................................................................................... 128
    **Spencer Spit State Park** .............................................................................. 131
    **Lopez Farm Cottages and Tent Camping** ................................................... 133
    **Hummel Lake** .............................................................................................. 134
    **Shark Reef Sanctuary** ................................................................................. 135
    **Agate Beach County Park** .......................................................................... 136
    **Iceberg point** ............................................................................................... 136
    **Mackaye Harbor Boat Launch** .................................................................... 137
    **Hunter Bay County Dock and Boat Ramp** .................................................. 137
    **Southend General Store and Restaurant** ................................................... 137
    **Otis Perkins Day Park** ................................................................................ 138
    **Islands Marine Center** ................................................................................ 139
    **Lopez Islander Resort Marina** .................................................................... 140
**Shaw Island - including map** ............................................................................... 141
**Victoria and Butchart Gardens** ............................................................................ 143
**Vancouver BC for Boaters - Quick Check Map on pg 144** ................................. 148
**Customs and Canada for Boaters only** ............................................................... 150
**Pump Out Locations** ........................................................................................... 151
**Larger Anchorages** ............................................................................................. 151
**Fuel and Grocery Stores on the Water** .............................................................. 152
**Launching Ramps** ............................................................................................... 154
**Kayak Day Paddles and Camping Trips** ............................................................. 156
**Kayaker and human or wind powered campsites and launch sites, Cascadia Marine Trail Sites** ............ 158
**John's over the top Packing List** ........................................................................ 160
**Urgent care - Emergency - Locations and Numbers** ......................................... 163
**Resources every boater in the San Juan's needs to know** ................................ 164
**Authors note - from me to you** ............................................................................ 165
**Mileage Chart** ...................................................................................................... 168

9

# WELCOME

Welcome to the San Juan's, just possibly the west coast's favorite destination. The San Juan Islands are located in the far northwest corner of Washington State sandwiched between Canada's Vancouver Island and Washington's mainland. The area is broadly known as the Salish Sea, and is named after the many groups and tribes of the indigenous Salish peoples.

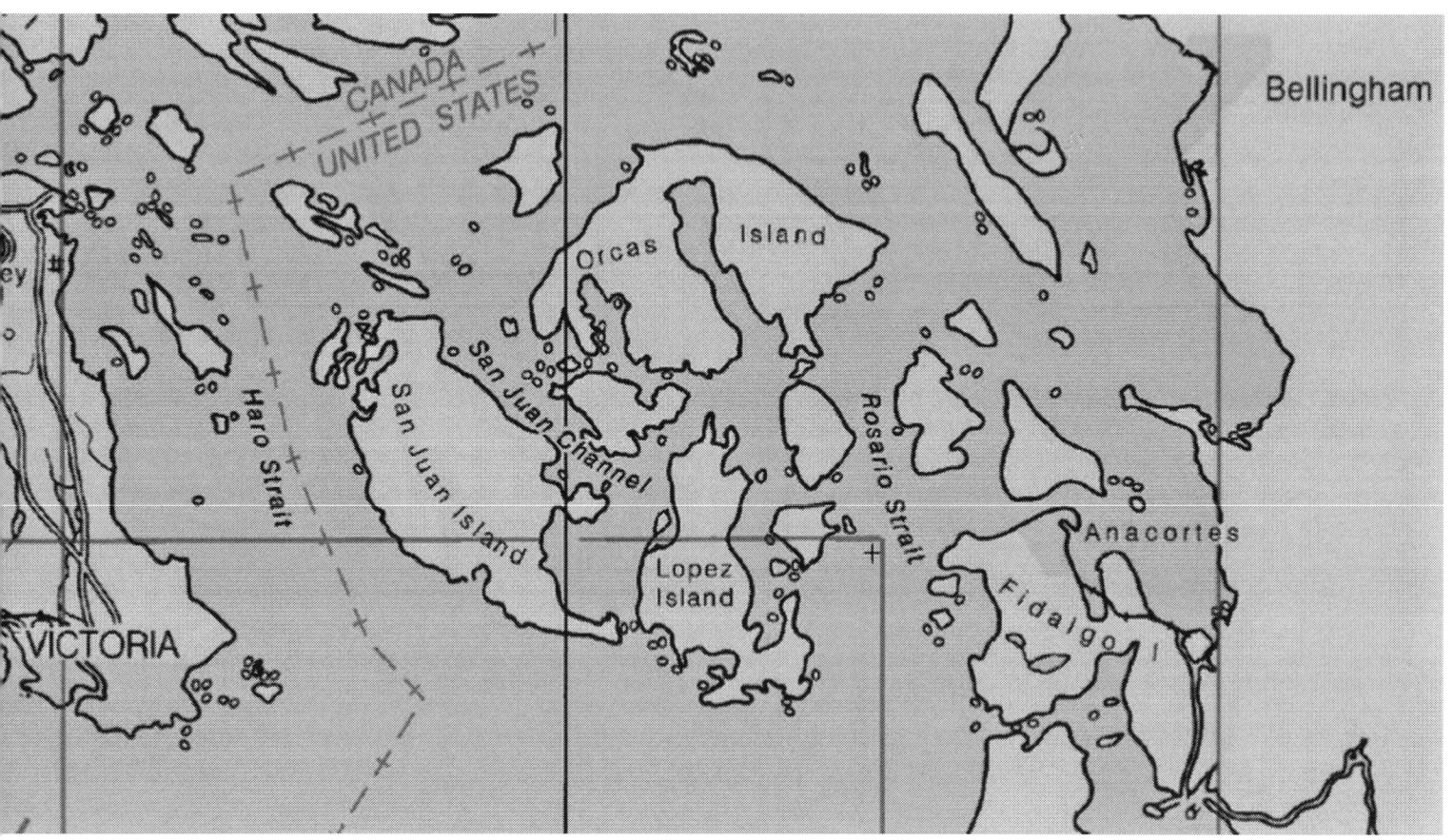

This *"Land and Sea"* guidebook is for all visitors. Whether you arrive by boat, car or bicycle, you will find just what you need for camping, hiking, kayaking, cruising or pedaling around the islands.

All publicly accessible San Juan Island city's, villages, resorts and marinas, plus the outer island marine parks are included.

For you to truly enjoy and experience the San Juan's you need to know about nearby attractions and resources, so included are more than the typical San Juan guidebook might cover.

Deception Pass, Anacortes, La Conner, Butchart Gardens, Victoria and Squalicum Harbor, are all reviewed with practical tips and useful advice.

# Using this Guidebook

Anacortes and Ferry travel to Friday Harbor and San Juan island are first. Next I picked out the nearby islands and moved pretty much in a clockwise fashion around the San Juans, jumping back and forth between boater only and car only discussions. At the beginning of the chapters about bigger islands I have included maps or charts with labels marking important details. The maps are followed by paragraphs explaining specific pertinent information.

When using the guidebook, you will want to keep coming back to the two page orientation map at the front, then using the table of contents find the pages you are interested in. For very specific items, look in the comprehensive index at the back for page numbers.

For trip planning, I suggest you do not plan a whirlwind vacation trying to do it all. Instead try to zero in on a few interests. For instance if whale (orca) watching or kayaking is what drives you, then get reservations at San Juan County Park on San Juan Island and make the campground your home base. If you are driven to distraction by the artsy crafty crowd, then get reservations at Moran State Park or West Beach Resort on Orcas Island, and hang out at Eastsound. If you are a biking and serenity solitude nut, perhaps Odlin County Park on Lopez Island will suit you best.

Once you have made an initial first night choice, I suggest you fill in with side excursions, and if time permits, island hop in a few days. Lastly, once situated, try to leave your car or boat behind and use the free inter-island ferry and inexpensive local transit for excursions. For instance, you can camp on Lopez Island and easily spend the day on foot or bicycle on San Juan Island in Friday Harbor shopping, or at Whale Watch Park orca viewing and be back at your campsite that night, all without getting in your car or driving the boat.

## About the San Juan's

The San Juan's consist of over seven hundred islands, islets and rocky clusters plus or minus depending on the changing tides, so it is not surprising that San Juan County is over seventy percent under water. Most residents live on the four largest islands served by state ferries, but smaller private islands and marine state parks accessible only by boat or airplane are plentiful.

## SHAW ISLAND

Shaw Island, the fourth largest, is completely residential. Except for a seasonal store at the ferry landing and eleven campsites and public beach at Shaw Island County Park, all the land is private. The ferry provides regular service for tourists and residents alike, but most day visitors simply drive or bicycle Shaw islands thirteen miles of public road and then board the next ferry.

## LOPEZ ISLAND

Number three in size is Lopez Island. Lopez is known for pastoral farmland, a laid-back population, great level bicycling and numerous parks. The main business district is Lopez Village where you will find grocery stores, boutiques, craft shops, galleries, and eateries. B&B's and vacation rentals abound on Lopez. Visiting boaters may anchor in nearby Idyllic Fisherman Bay or one of the parks. Fisherman Bay is home to a full service marina and a destination resort complete with cabins, RV and tenting sites and its own moorage. A state park and a county park offer waterfront camping while several day parks provide visitors access to picturesque vistas and beaches. Lopez is somewhat long and skinny with roads crisscrossing as well as running end-to-end creating bicycling and driving loops from short to all day outings. Over the years, locals have promoted a friendly welcome attitude by waving at cars, bicycles and pedestrians. The longstanding tradition is firmly entrenched and visitors soon join in, returning waves and smiles.

## SAN JUAN ISLAND

San Juan Island is number two in size and home to the city of Friday Harbor. Friday Harbor is the only incorporated city in the San Juan's and the San Juan County seat. The Port of Friday Harbor maintains a very large first class marina drawing mariners from around the world. Both commercial and private airplanes use the nearby airport. Float equipped seaplanes land in the protected harbor taxiing to a dock reserved for them. A short pedestrian esplanade runs along the waterfront connecting the marina, downtown and the ferry terminal. On busy days, up to 150 vehicles per ferry are unloaded and loaded. There may be a dozen ferries each day. San Juan Island is home to state parks, county parks, and resorts catering to visitors arriving by air, boat, car, on foot and many—riding bicycles. Being the commercial hub of the islands brings San Juan Island lots of traffic, lots of people, and with it the inevitable hustle and bustle. Unlike Lopez, few people wave and horn honking is not unheard of on San Juan Island. There are no bike lanes, bicyclists and drivers share the road and frustrations, but when all is said and done—Friday Harbor and San Juan Island is the heart of the islands, and not to be missed.

## ORCAS ISLAND

Orcas Island, just barely squeaks out San Juan as the largest Island of the San Juan's. Orcas has a distinctive horseshoe shape, and arguably the most name recognition. The large ferry lanes waiting area attests to Orcas Island's popularity. Visitors are advised by Washington's department of transportation to have advance ferry reservations during the busy summer month's or risk missing the boat and waiting for the next one. Like San Juan, Orcas has only one city, unincorporated Eastsound. There are a number of resorts, marinas, and B&B's scattered from one end of the nearly 60 square mile island to the other end, but Eastsound is the only genuine city. Affectionately referred to as a village, Eastsound is confusingly located at the far end of East Sound, the waterway. Orcas Island is home to popular Moran State Park and the tallest point in the San Juan Islands, 2400 ft high Mt. Constitution. Orcas Island is the hilliest of the San Juan's and the furthest end-to-end. Tossing in narrow, sometimes-dark tree lined roads makes Orcas Island a challenge for drivers and cyclists sharing the roads.

## OUTER ISLANDS and other Places

The rest of the San Juan Islands and area attractions consist of private islands with no public access and lots of State Marine Parks, many occupying an entire island. The ferry system only serves the four largest islands leaving the rest to be reached by private shuttles, water taxis, airplanes and of course residents and visitors in their own boats.

**Marine Parks and Destinations**

| | |
|---|---|
| Jones | Posey |
| James | Hope |
| Stuart | Skagit |
| Sucia | Goat |
| Patos | Turn |
| Matia | Doe |
| Clark | Deception Pass |
| Cypress | Butchart Gardens |
| Saddlebag | Victoria |

# Gateway to the San Juans — Finding Anacortes

*I*t is not difficult to get to the San Juans, most people go by ferry and all the ferries depart from the city of Anacortes, WA. Anacortes is about two hours north of Seattle and thirty minutes west of the I-5 freeway. For those of you hauling the family boat up the freeway, you have several choices. You may launch at Anacortes or go to one of five choices at other locations (see boat ramp section)

When traveling north on the freeway, there are only two exit choices you should consider, exit #221, and exit #230. The first exit is #221 and says "La Conner." Nine miles further is heavily used exit #230 and the sign says "To Anacortes and Ferries." Both roads are excellent and suitable for towing the family yacht, but the La Conner route saves about 2-3 miles, and might be faster due to less traffic. When taking the La Conner route, you will not actually drive into La Conner unless you want to. Simply stay on *Best Rd* until you turn left on hwy 20 rejoining the ferry and Anacortes traffic.

🎯 Snack **Tip:** On the La Conner route – you will go right by a large fruit stand with huge craft ice cream cones and a convenient restroom. Need I say more?

Check for seasonal seafood at *Snow Goose* Produce fruit stand market on the way to La Conner.

🎯 **Tip:** I suggest that you allow time to visit historic La Conner sometime on your trip, even a short half hour walk along the waterfront is well worth it.

## La Conner Waterfront

Waterfront esplanade and visiting boater overnight docks at La Conner.
(See the La Conner chapter)

La Conner is a working fishing and lumber processing city, but at the same time, embraces the boating, tourist and arts community.

*Safeway before ferry terminal*

Once you make it to Anacortes, regardless of the exit or route you follow, you will be on the main road into town. You won't have any secret turns or problems finding your way. You will still be on hwy 20, but the road signs will now say Commercial Ave. Keep going about a mile and turn left on 12th st. at the sign saying **"Ferries."** There is a Safeway on the corner of 12th and Commercial, (where you turn) this will be your last chance to stock up before getting on the ferry. The ferry terminal is only ten minutes further. (3 ½ miles) FYI – Cap Sante Marina is conveniently located across the next street over from Safeway and West Marine is in the next block.

## The Anacortes Ferry Terminal

*F*orty five to sixty minutes before the next ferry sails, the road from town to the ferry terminal fill with cars in a hurry. It seems everyone suddenly has to catch the next boat. Get in line with the rest, you won't miss the entrance turn off, it's where everyone is going. Chances are you have already spotted the waiting ferry. Traffic lines up single file and then splits into four ticket booth lines. They are all the same, pick a lane with a green light turned on.

Bring cash or credit/debit cards but *no personal checks.* As of 2016, they took travelers checks but I would verify that before leaving home.

**Tip: Yes, they take reservations.** You would be smart to go online before you leave home and secure your sailing time slot. If you don't and the ferry is full you will have to sit in line until the next ferry boards, costing you potentially a few hours or even over night.

The ticketing process goes fast if you don't pester the attendant with trivial questions. Even faster if you have your printed reservation in hand. **DO IT!** After paying, the attendant will point you to the proper waiting lane, e.g. lane 5 for Orcas, lane 12 for Lopez. Once in your assigned waiting lane shut off the motor and relax. You can get out and walk around, take the dog on a leash over to the side. There are bathrooms nearby.

🎯 **Tip** There is a café and foot passenger waiting area. You and your passengers may hang out at the cafe if you are early. The ferry crew will direct you when loading, once parked, you may stay in your car or lock up and go upstairs. The view from high on a ferry is not to be missed. Some of the ferries are very big with up to two hundred cars on two levels and two passenger decks. Pay attention to where you are parked, it's easy to  temporarily lose your car and your people, and the first stop at Lopez Landing is in less than an hour.

**One long blast** of the whistle signals the ferry is under way. A low rumble and vibration flows through the ship – a glance out the windows verify's you are moving.

**Warp, Woof, Woof**

A warp and two woof's, also known as a long and two short blasts of the whistle is how some captains will announce the ferries arrival. This traditional signal originated back in the steam whistle days when the whistle was blown by pulling on a cord modulating the sound. Many captains developed their own unique signature whistle sound. Today, the warp and two woofs are still in use if you listen but the distinctive steam whistle sound is gone forever. You may also hear five or more rapid short whistle blasts warning a wayward boater to steer clear. Not everyone gets warned, one day we watched as a becalmed small sail-boater rowed feverishly to get out of the way of our approaching ferry. Our captain rather than terrify the hapless boater, slowed and went around.

17

Foot passengers and bicyclists are first on and first off.

## Getting off the Ferry

By now you should feel at home and have explored the ferry from end to end and top to bottom. As you approach the terminals at Lopez, Shaw, Orcas or Friday Harbor, someone will make an announcement saying for departing foot passengers to assemble on the car deck and drivers to return to their cars. There will be no second announcement, even though the ferry is still underway you need to get to your car. Foot passengers and cyclists will walk off first, unloading will begin within seconds of the ramp being lowered. I recommend on your first ferry ride that your passengers ride in the car when disembarking because everyone will be coming off single file and drive away in a hurry. It could be several blocks before you can pull over to pick them up. Having everyone in the car is a good way to make sure they don't forget to get off.

 Tips about the Ferries of the San Juan's

- You only pay fare going westward (everywhere outbound from Anacortes is westward.) So it is a free ride coming back, even if you didn't arrive by ferry
- Friday Harbor is the furthest and the most fare, if you go to Lopez, Orcas or Shaw it will be less, but then if you decide to continue on (on to Friday Harbor) the next day or even the same day, you will have to pay a little more.
- When you ride eastward, (to Anacortes) you can get off on any of the other three islands, (free stop over's) and then later (any day), get back on still going eastward for free.
- Foot passengers and cyclists may ride inter-island, east or west "free." This means, once in the islands, foot passengers with bikes may travel back and forth between islands as easy as walking on the ferry. Kayaks are charged a nominal fee westward only.

18

- I suggest if you are a biking around, that you make one island your home base and then ride to other islands for day trips. Remember, the ferry is free and cyclists get on first and off first.
- There are no big waiting lines for foot passengers so there is no need to arrive early, but don't be even one minute late. The ferries are punctual and don't wait unless the crew hears you screaming while you're running down the ramp flapping your arms.
- Yes, you can carry kayaks on board, wait in the passenger/bicycle area, and the loading crew will direct you where to go, but when going westward check with ticketing in case they charge you for your kayak.
- Be ready to load, especially for inter-island jaunts. I have been on ferries that have loaded and pulled away from the dock in nine minutes. Punctual? — Yes.
- Study the ferry schedule online at wsdot – It is confusing at first but actually make sense once you read it several times.

 http://www.wsdot.com/ferries/schedule/ScheduleDetailByRoute.aspx?route=ana-sj-sid

FYI - The 2016 fare for car and driver to Friday Harbor was $63.75, each passenger $13.25, under eighteen $6.60, bicycles $4.00 ea. Off season is less.

Long RV's and travel trailers are considerably more expensive, see rates at wsdot. (web site above)

Note: The Anacortes terminal has lots and lots of parking for commuters and people that go as foot and bicycle passengers. Many people bike camping and kayaking the San Juan's will leave their cars for a week or two while they explore. The parking fee varies with time length.

**Park and Go
makes great sense for
bikers and kayakers.**

— Best times to travel on the ferry —

Wsdot has published the below suggestions for travel. This excerpt is from their web site.

*Visitors, vacationers and commuters will be vying for limited car deck space for their vehicles, especially in July and August. Busiest travel times are Thursday and Friday Evenings westbound, and Sunday afternoons eastbound. In the San Juan's, peak travel times from Anacortes are Thursday and Friday afternoons and Saturday mornings. Peak travel times from the islands are all day Sunday and Monday morning.*

# Bringing Your Boat to the San Juan's

$\mathcal{B}$oating the San Juan's opens a vastly larger area normally not visited by the land bound tourist in a car. The ferry system provides access to the four largest islands, but that leaves dozens of marine parks and preserves available only by private boat. Going by boat is more than exploring waterways and quiet coves; it frees the traveler from needing reservations and dealing with traffic and parking and yes, at times, congested ferries. Virtually all attractions, villages and resorts are available to boaters, albeit sometimes it takes a little work; even creativity on the part of the boater to get to places when their primary transportation is tied to a dock, or anchored offshore.

This is the Squalicum Harbor ramp in Bellingham.   **Tip: I recommend you put in here.**

## Getting in Salty Water:

Few to zero visitors trailer their boats on a ferry, and I don't recommend you consider doing it either. Not only does it complicate things immensely, it is just not sensible for most of us. Island ramps, public and private, are woefully inadequate and few. Trailer parking will be day use only. An exception may be if you are planning an extended visit and have land based lodging set up. For instance, some private resorts offer shallow beach ramps for guests. Kayaks are another matter; it makes very good sense to bring kayaks by car. Not surprisingly, many boaters carry kayaks on their boats. Your best bet is to splash your yacht at one of half a dozen marinas or ramps on the mainland and then run the twenty or so miles to the island or marine park of your choice.

## Boat Ramps - Travel lifts

There are six choices where to launch, each with plus and minuses. All the ramps listed have floats for short-term use while launching or retrieving your boat. They all have long-term parking.

- Cap Sante Marina in Anacortes has a sling and travel lift (no ramp), plus long-term fee parking. Transient boater moorage is available (drop in, or with reservation).

- Washington Park in Anacortes has a two-lane ramp and long term fee parking. The park has a nice forested campground that may figure into your plans. Campground reservations are recommended during summer months. You may not overnight at the ramp float but anchoring is easy.

- Cornet Bay at Deception Pass State Park has a four-lane ramp and acres of fee parking. Transient boater docks are next to ramp, plus there is room for anchoring.

- Squalicum Harbor Marina in Bellingham has a four-lane ramp with lots of FREE parking, plus fresh water wash down hoses.

**Tip:** Squalicum is the best place to launch, and transient boater docks are available too.

- La Conner on Swinomish Channel has a one-lane city ramp and float and overnight fee parking. The La Conner Marina (Port of Skagit County) has a 5000 pound sling and several nearby yards have travel lifts. Transient boater docks are available along the esplanade and at the marina.

- Twin Bridges is a two-lane ramp and metered parking. Provided by Skagit County on Swinomish Channel (where hwy 20 crosses Swinomish Channel) **Tip: Use Twin Bridges with caution.** The ramps are unusable at lower tides, the current is problematic, parking security is questionable, and the restrooms overused.

**On the upside** – Kayakers will find Twin Bridges is perfect for running Swinomish channel.

That's it! – **That's all** of the nearby area ramps for jumping off to the San Juans.

21

## Notes About Ramps and Travel Lifts

- Expect sand and slippery seaweed on the ramps. My heavy boats sometimes require 4x4 to get up the hill.
- Expect currents, wind and waves, and prepare your crew with appropriate lines or risk watching them get pulled in wrestling to control the boat.
- Do not expect any yard or marina to hoist your boat without prior reservation, and expect your reservation to get pushed back due to earlier problems. End of the day reservations are risky if your trip plan is tightly scheduled.
- 🎯 **Tip** – allow plenty of time for yard launching and retrieval. Schedule in the <u>am</u> if possible. Using a ramp solves a lot of issues, but dumps the trailer in salt water.
- If possible, you should hose down your trailer asap after dunking, not two weeks later when you get home, but home is better than not at all.
- At all ramps and yards, plan to move your boat away from immediate area right away so others may launch.
- Be sure to inform yard beforehand if you are launching a sailboat and need the mast stepped, some yards don't step masts, or charge extra.
- All ramps listed have level staging areas where you can rig and self step masts
- I know of no place (none) where there is a spar, or do-it-yourself tackle for standing masts. You are on your own. Thanks for asking.

### Choices - Choices - Choices

I use all the ramps except Twin Bridges, but I would go back there again if I had a compelling reason. My point is, even though I suggest you go to Squalicum Harbor, it may be best for you to start at Cornet Bay, or somewhere else, it all depends on where you are going and what you plan on doing. I admit I like the free parking in Bellingham and I visit my brother on Lummi Island.

If you plan to fish or sail the Strait of Juan De Fuca and camp at Deception Pass, then put in at Cornet Bay. If you are going to Echo Bay on Sucia first thing, and you are worried about possible pea soup fog down south, then head for Squalicum Harbor.

If the worst thing in the world is to dunk your brand new non-galvanized trailer in salt water, then have Cap Sante Marina hoist your treasure in for you.

*The choice of where to launch ought to be easy once the big picture comes into focus.*

# San Juan Island - Friday Harbor

$A$sk me—"What is the one place I recommend a visitor to the San Juan's visit, if they only have one day and one stop." My first thought is, "What a dumb plan," and then I think Friday Harbor, hands down, there is no other choice.

*Looking up Spring St (main street) from the turn around esplanade.*

When driving off the ferry you must drive up Spring St so there is always a little congestion when the boat unloads, but the crowd quickly dissipates into the town and countryside. When you first arrive in Friday Harbor, by boat or on the ferry, the first thing you need to do is get out of the car or off your yacht and stand somewhere on the waterfront esplanade. Let the ambience of an old robust seafaring town wash over you. Listen to the gulls, the street musicians and nautical noises unique of an active working harbor. Watch the tourists, wide eyed taking it all in.

Once properly acclimated, you should take a walking tour. I suggest that you walk both directions on the esplanade first. If you came by ferry, stroll out on the docks, if you came by boat, go look at the ferry terminal and watch a four hundred footer pull in as easy as you would park your car.

# San Juan Island — Quick Check

Roche Harbor Resort - 248 Reuben Mem. Dr 98250
(360) 378-2155 - Marina - 1-800-586-3590

San Juan Islands Sculpture Park - 9083 Roche Harbor Dr. 98250 (360) 370-0035

Posey Island State Park
Address: Pearl Island, Friday Harbor, Wa 98250
(360) 378-2044

Rueben Tarte County Park - San Juan Dr - cross st Limestone Point Rd- (GPS) N48 36.743, W123 5.914

English Camp - West Valley Rd, Friday Harbor, WA. 98250 (360) 378-2240

Krystal Acres Alapaca Farm and Country Store
3501 West Valley Rd 98250 (360) 378-6125

Lakedale Resort - 4313 Roche Harbor Rd , Friday Harbor WA 98250 (360) 378-2350

San Juan County Park - 50 San Juan Park Dr - 98250 (360) 378 8420 (at Smallpox Bay)

Lime Kiln Point State Park (aka) Whale Watch Park 1567 Westside Rd - 98250 (360) 378-2044 - Interpretive Center and friends of Lime Kiln Society (360) 378-5154 special programs

Pelindaba Lavender Farm 45 Hawthorne Ln Friday harbor WA 98250

Eagle Cove - County day use Park - Eagle Cove Rd, Friday Harbor, WA 98250
GPS N48 31.718 W122 58.827 - (360) 378-8420

American Camp - 4668 Cattle Point Rd, Friday Harbor WA 98250 (360) 378-2240 < seven miles from Friday Harbor

Cattle Point Lighthouse - Location - southern end of San Juan Island, near end of Cattle Point Rd. - past American Camp

Fourth of July Beach and Jackals Lagoon have separate parking lots on north side of Cattle Point Rd, past American camp but before Cattle Pass Lighthouse. (GPS) 48.4680° N, 123.0032° W

Jackson Beach - Location - off Pear Point Rd between Argyle Ave. and Turn Point Rd. (GPS) 48.5198° N, 123.0110° W

Turn Point day use park is located on Turn Point Rd where Pinedrona Ln intersects < two miles from Friday Harbor (GPS N48° 31.718, W122° 58.827).

🎯 TIP: Do yourself a major favor and get a road map. The maps in this guidebook are meant to give you a leg up in your travels, not direct you down a lonely forest lane.

**Triple A** - AAA has them free to members , search AAA maps or call 1-800-444-8091

*Now a plug for Triple A - We joined when we began hauling trailers on road trips. We expanded our benefits to include children away at school. We have actually cashed in a few times near home and far away.*

*The convenience when we needed help is not measurable, the peace of mind when I hear a bump, thump or misfire can't be bought, and yet I did buy peace of mind, and I'm going to keep on buying it.*

That's my opinion - John

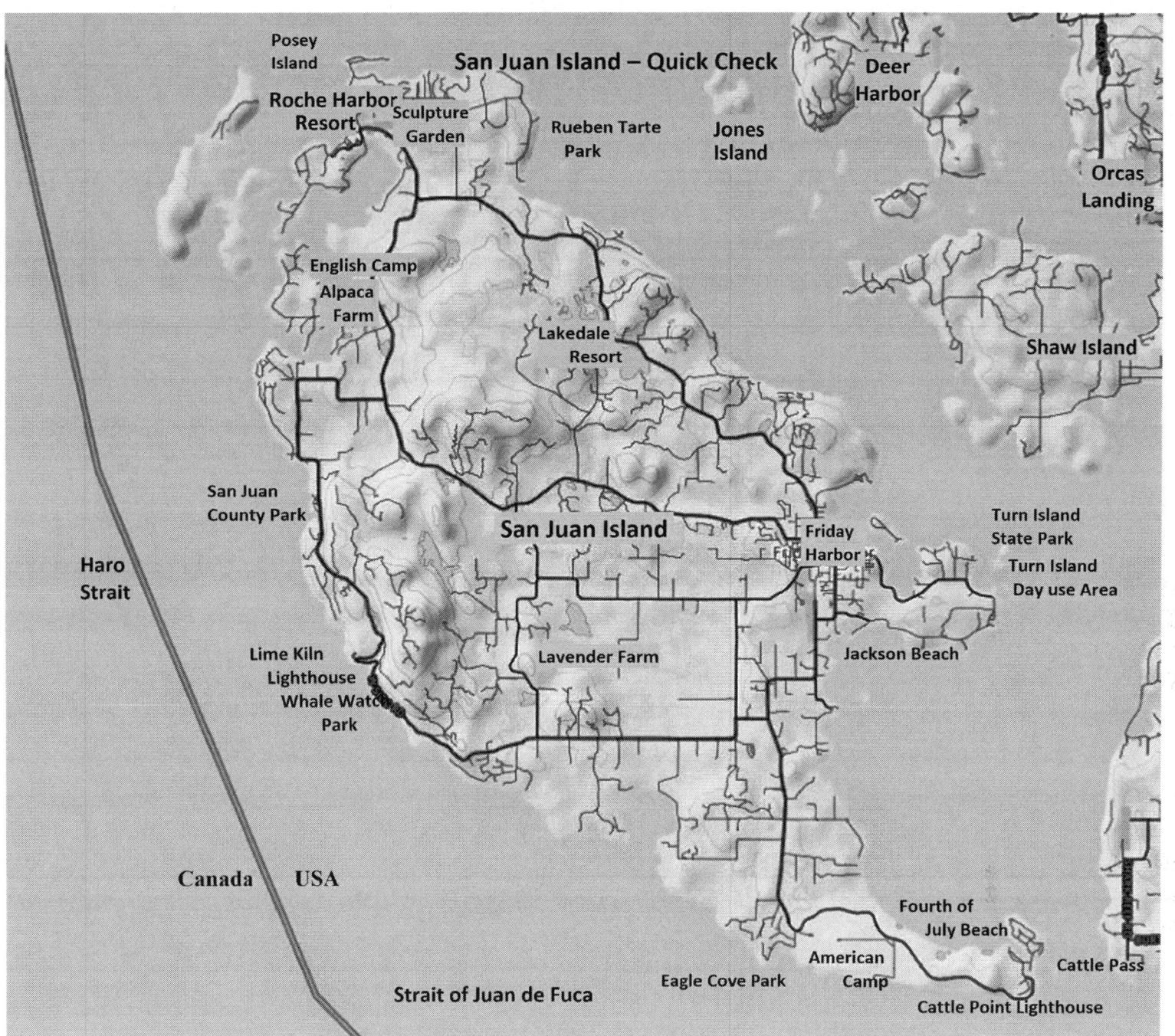

There are only three places offering camping on San Juan Island
1. San Juan County Park
2. Lakedale Resort
3. San Juan County Fairground in Friday Harbor (RV'S Only - no tents)

### San Juan Island Transit stops
Friday Harbor ferry – American Camp – Lavender Farm – Lime Kiln/Whale Watch Park – SJ County Park
Snug Harbor Resort – Krystal Acres Alpacas – English Camp – Sculpture Park
Roche Harbor Resort – Lakedale Resort – San Juan Vineyard

### The Transit runs daily on San Juan Island - but only May thru Sept.
- See schedule with p/u times here -
http://www.sanjuantransit.com/San%20Juan%20Island%20Summer%202016%20Transit%20Schedule.pdf

Partial view of the boat basin, transient docks are at far left, monthly slips on right. This is a big place; it's nearly a third mile from the outer breakwater to land when going for a dog walk.

**Tip**: Salt water aquarium. Spring Street is the main street that runs up and down the hill and ends at the waterfront esplanade with a little turnaround. At the foot of Spring St opposite the turn around memorial park, is a wharf that extends straight out. At the end of the wharf is the waiting terminal (Smallish building) for the *Victoria Clipper* passenger ferry. Inside is a big salt water aquarium and displays explaining what's living and growing under the sea. This is also a good place to watch ferries and tour boats come and go, seaplanes too.

Once you have the waterfront figured out, it is time to head uphill, walk any street, alley, or stairway. You will be pleasantly surprised at the number of little boutique shops, eateries and twisty malls tucked into about ten square blocks. Friday Harbor is full of secrets; each time I walk around I notice something special, neat or new.

Kings Market is the islands full size grocery and is two blocks up Spring St. on the right. The Saturday Farmers Market and public restrooms are across from Kings Market, but behind some buildings, cut through a passage (alley) or walk around and come in behind the Brickworks building.

Another block up Spring St. and you will come to a couple gas stations. Don't leave town without enough gas to get back. I don't think you will find fuel anywhere except Roche Harbor. The island is small by some standards but you still don't want to walk back.

The Whale Museum is a must for orca watchers.
Find it at 62 First St. The long stairway at the west end of the esplanade takes you almost directly to the door.

I would be remiss to leave out our best friends.

It's at 1011 Mullis St, which happens to be the same road you will take to American Camp.

My daughter walks from her boat, it's about one mile one way.

Eddie & Friends Dog Park

# Friday Harbor Marina

The port of Friday Harbor runs an immaculate premier destination marina for boaters. The port is the center of commerce for the San Juan's, and with the adjacent ferry terminal, boaters and non boaters converge on the city.

The marina boasts 500 slips and over 150 transient spaces. Broad concrete floats provide a labyrinth of walkways connecting with the outer breakwater more than a quarter mile from shore. Electricity, fresh water, fuel, ice, pump outs, and services are all available.

Out on the docks are convenient restrooms, and at the top of the gangplank are showers.

The breakwater floats are always open for the casual drop in boater that needs a restroom stop or has to run into town for groceries.

Kings Market is so close you can run for eggs before the coffee is done.

If you plan on spending the night simply radio the harbor master for a slip assignment on 66A or call them at 360 378 2688.

They take reservations for holidays, but the rest of the year they aren't needed. If you want to save boat dollars you can anchor close by and paddle over to the dinghy dock.

The "on the water" Fourth of July fireworks celebration rivals Roche Harbor and the city goes all out with a parade and picnic.

Some boaters will make Friday Harbor their home port for a week or more, venturing to the outer islands in the daytime and coming back to their waiting slip each night.

 **Tip – spend at least two nights here, you won't regret it!**

Boats and boardwalks - what every skipper secretly desires.

# Friday Harbor Marina Map

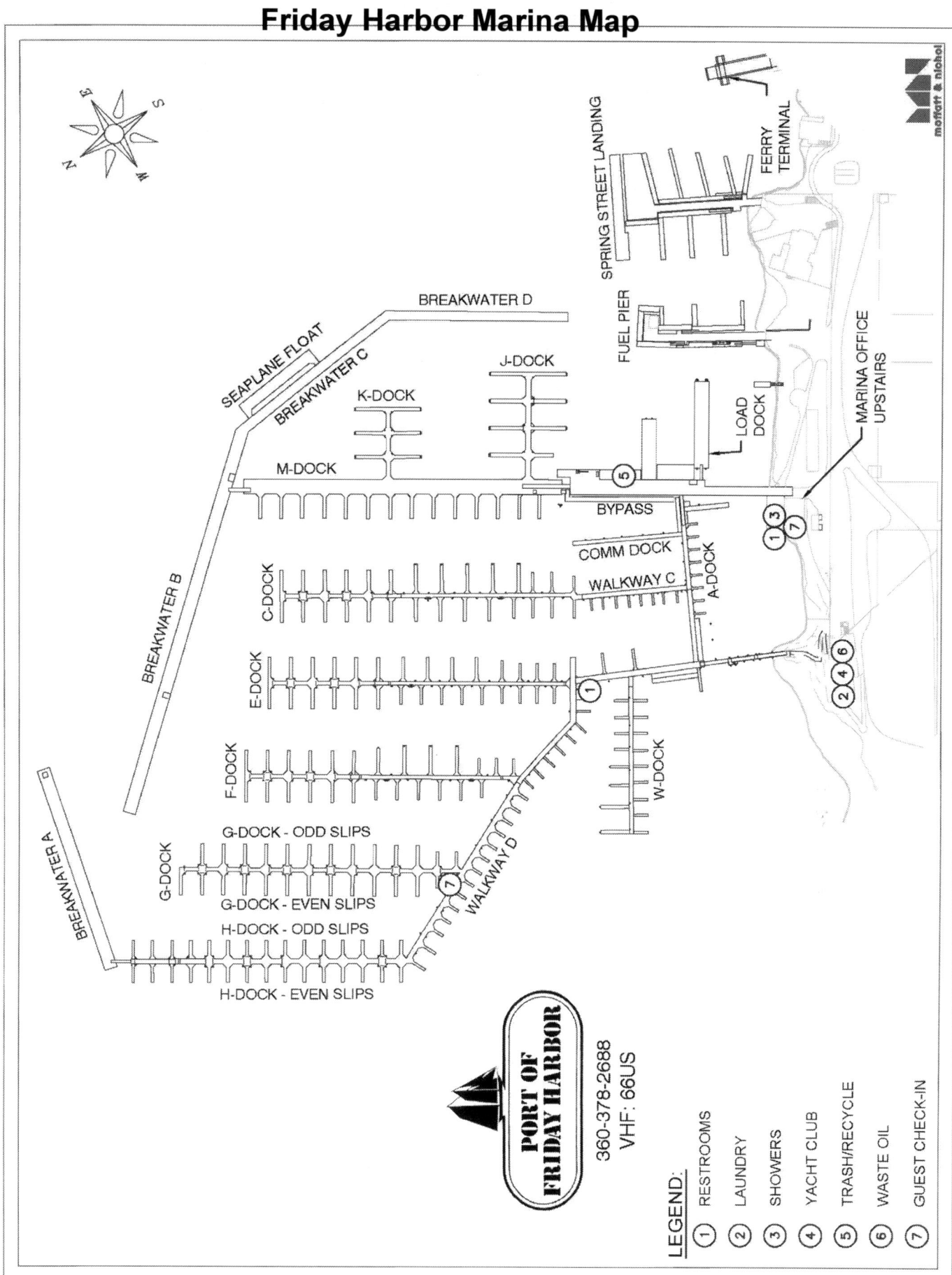

Image courtesy of the Port of Friday Harbor

# Friday Harbor Downtown Area

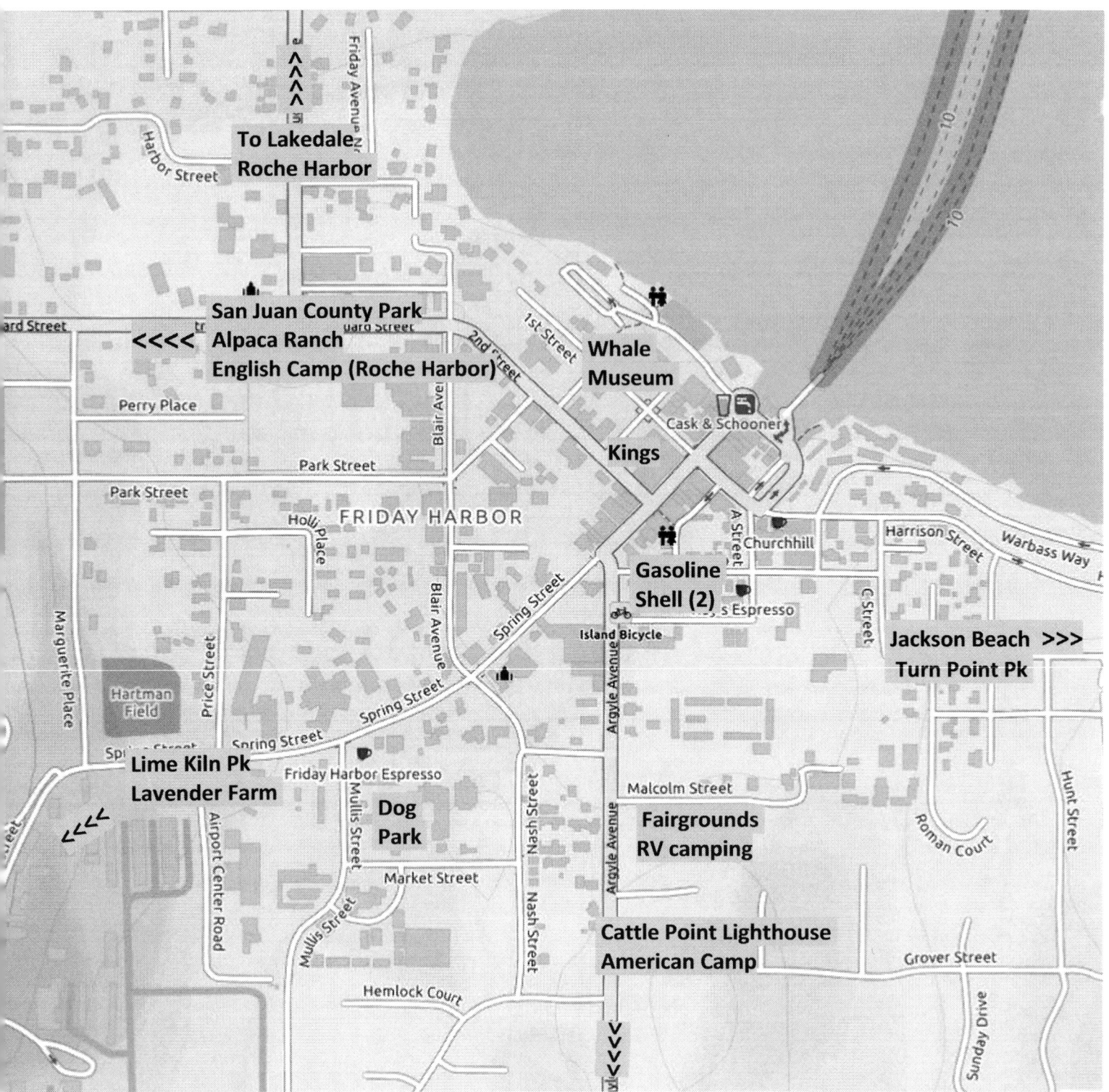

**Marked on map are the roads leading to:**
- Roche Harbor
- Lakedale Resort
- English Camp
- Alpaca Ranch
- SJ County Park
- Lime Kiln Park
- Lavender Farm
- Cattle Point
- American Camp
- Jackson Beach
- Turn Pt Park

**Also marked are:**
- Whale museum
- Dog Park
- Kings Market
- Gasoline station
- Fairgrounds

**Tip: "Catch the "San Juan Island Transit"**

Look for the "Transit Sign," next to the ferry waiting lanes. Check online for the up to date schedule with times and stops for the blue line and green line at **http://www.sanjuantransit.com/schedules.html** or call 360 378 8887  Van buses run daily, May 20th to Oct 6th (2016) (Orcas and Lopez dates differ)

It's not too early to be making plans for your trip to the San Juan's.
Part of making workable plans is knowing what your options are.  If all you want to do is sit on your boat or park your car at a resort, then stop right now.
If, on the other hand you think about what new excursions wait you – keep reading.

Did you know that San Juan Transit runs a "Sunset Viewing Tour" from Friday Harbor to Lime Kiln/Whale Watch Park?  It takes about an hour.  Be at the Friday Harbor bus stop (by the ferry lanes) ¾ hour before sunset - don't be late!
Did you know that you can ride your bicycle to any point they service and then come back on the little bus if you are too tuckered to ride back?  Five bucks, and if it's raining, still five bucks.

San Juan Transit carries bicycles on the front and if they have more, they bring them inside.
One way fare is $5, all day is $15, two day is $25. And it's good on the other islands too.

With a little creative outside the box thinking and free inter-island (passenger and bicycle) ferry service, you can expand your horizons.  Sit down with a ferry and transit schedule and see what you can come up with.  (they are both online)

 Here's a bike hike idea. Start out by riding your two wheeler from Friday Harbor to American Camp.
Next, hop the transit over the mountain to English Camp, then ride to Roche Harbor, and then catch the transit back to Friday Harbor. Tomorrow morning with your bike, catch the ferry to Lopez and, you get the idea!

## San Juan Island Transit Bus Stops

Check web site above for spring , summer, and fall pick up and drop off times at below stops.
- Friday Harbor ferry
- American Camp
- Lavender Farm
- Lime Kiln/Whale Watch  Park
- SJ County Park
- Snug Harbor Resort
- Krystal Acres Alpacas
- English Camp
- Sculpture Park
- Roche Harbor Resort
- Lakedale Resort
- San Juan Vineyard

# RV Camping at the Fairgrounds in Friday Harbor

Camping at the Fairground

Where to park the coach for the night is always the problem when traveling. Coming to a small county circled by water makes it worse. San Juan County Fairground offers eight RV sites with water and electricity hook ups only. Tent camping is forbidden. The sites are in a row to one side on a grassy field. On site are restrooms, a playground and a skateboard park. No black/gray waste dumping at the fairground, but just down the road at 375 Tucker Ave. is a waste dump facility. There are no fire pits but you can use your propane barbecue. Dogs are allowed on leash only. Drop in RV camping is open year around but the bathrooms may be closed in the off season. The address is 846 Argyle Ave. Argyle is off Spring St three blocks up from the ferry landing. You would be wise to secure a reservation during summer months or when events are scheduled.

Contact: info@sjcfair.org or call the park office at 360 378 8420

There are a few private parties on the island offering tent and RV space, but in the interest of not publishing dated or useless obsolete information, they are beyond the purview of this guidebook.

Below is the picnic shelter - RV sites are to right off camera.

# Turn Island State Park & Turn Point Day Use Area

Some astute readers may be going, wait a minute how can a day use area be an island. Simple, they are two different places. The island is a state park a quarter mile offshore, the day use area is a county park on San Juan Island.

Boaters and kayakers will find **Turn Island** on their charts one and a half miles east of Friday Harbor right on the corner where all water traffic must **Turn** when heading to or from San Juan Channel and ultimately Cattle Pass.

Turn Island is an excellent kayaker destination and sports a dozen campsites. If your mother ship is in a slip at Friday Harbor, Turn Island is a comfortable shore hugging dinghy ride away. There are two anchor buoys and easy anchoring. The cove is a nice gravel dinghy friendly beach.

The smallish 35 acre island is ringed with an easy trail you can walk in thirty minutes or less. If you listen during flood and ebb, you can hear noisy fast water coming from the rocky shallows on the east side. Not to worry—the west side is fine for boating.

🎯 **Tip  Local knowledge**

**T**urn Point Day Use Area is on the mainland almost directly opposite it's namesake island. It is unlikely you will spot it from off shore unless you know exactly where to look.

To find the day use area from Friday Harbor take Spring St up the hill and turn left on 1st street, follow 1st until it becomes Harrison, follow Harrison it becomes Turn Point Rd, follow Turn Point Rd until you are about two miles from Friday Harbor and on your left will be a small street named Pinedrona Ln. Right at the Pinedrona sign is a little gravel drive that goes straight ahead for one hundred feet and into a twenty car parking lot. There is no street sign except the Pinedrona sign, but the parking lot has park rules and regulation signs so you will know for sure you are in the

Turn Island viewed from Turn Point Day Use Area

correct place. The trail to the beach is only a hundred feet or so and the private land on both sides of the hundred foot wide public beach are well marked.

This is a perfect place to park your car and launch kayaks for a quick quarter mile paddle to Turn Island. For me - I just run the dinghy over from my slip at Friday Harbor, that way I can look at the nice waterfront homes along the way.

**Note:** It is typical that there are no signs showing the way to public beaches in San Juan County. The state does a fair job of marking things for tourists, but the county day use areas, not so well.

# Lafarge Open Space

 **Tip - Local knowledge**

*I* like driving and cycling in circles, that way I end up back where I belong without repeating scenery or having to climb killer hills I just coasted down. (I know there's a basic flaw in my hill logic)

For this reason let's continue on Turn Point Rd and see where it leads us.

Turn Point Rd becomes Pear Point Rd and after about 2 miles of forest and country estates you will come to a bluff above North Bay and San Juan channel. With some squinting you can see all the way to Cattle Pass. Lafarge Open Space is on the right side. There is a gravel pullover, the Lafarge sign, and a fence that looks like it is for horses, but is really to keep out bicycles.

When the Lafarge gravel operation ceased, they gave their old pit to the parks district to become a park. And so it sits ready for development, but in the meantime it has been opened for hiking and dog walking. Nice graded paths circle the rim. Dogs may be off leash, but bicycles must be hitched outside. There is no water or shade or restroom.

# Jackson Beach Park

Across from the Lafarge Open Space and down a block, but still on Pear Point Rd is Jackson Beach Park. This is a day use area with a good boat ramp and float. It's the only public ramp I know of on San Juan Island that's useable. There's a ramp at Roche Harbor but it is always locked up making me wonder.

Other than a restroom by the ramp there's nothing here but driftwood and picnicking. The beach is a **lee shore** on San Juan Channel and by way of Cattle Pass, an extension of the Strait of Juan De Fuca. Old salty boaters know what that means (lee shore). It means there will be storm tossed logs and flotsam piled high from winter storms. Have fun scavenging.

Jackson Beach Park - The boat ramp is off to the right.
There is day use trailer parking and a float beside the ramp.

🎯 Tip  When you are on the ferry, grab a free tourist map from the ferry map rack.

## American Camp

You can't learn about American Camp without learning about English Camp.  Then inevitably out comes the Pig War and the twelve year standoff between the US and Great Britain.  The argument over the border and who own the San Juan Islands had been growing for years but was civilized and peaceful.  The rhetoric escalated when a wayward English pig was shot when caught rooting around in the garden of an American farmer.  I'll leave the rest for you to learn on your own.

American Camp is located out on the barren windswept southern end of San Juan Island overlooking Haro strait and Cattle Pass.  It was a defensive military location, not somewhere most people would choose to live.  Each time I visit, I think about how miserable it must have been for the American soldiers garrisoned there.

From Friday Harbor drive up the main street (Spring St) and turn left just before the airport. (Mullis St) Mullis becomes  Cattle Point Rd and you are on your way, its about 6 miles or so.  You may also turn left on Argyle and follow it over to Cattle Point Rd.  🎯 **Tip: -** Don't rely on street signs to point the way. San Juan County marks most road names at intersections, but arrows and signs directing to parks are conspicuously absent.

37

American Camp has an interpretive center and of course miles of trails leading to plaques and places where the US army had encamped and set up quarters. There are trailheads to Jackles Lagoon, Fourth of July Beach, Pickett's Monument and more. If you want punishment you can walk all the way to Cattle Point Light, but I would drive. I think at a minimum you should visit the American Camp interpretive center. Also check out the new interpretive center down the road at Cattle Point. The view is spectacular.

I have ridden my bicycle from the marina at Friday Harbor, to American Camp, Cattle Point Light and back. It's an enjoyable fifteen mile ride and not too hilly outing that's guaranteed to improve your appetite and promise a good night's sleep.

FYI – While you might be able to land your dinghy and find American Camp by boat, take it from me, I have tried. It is much more difficult than it seems and definitely not worth the effort. If you visit American Camp, you must also visit English Camp to see the other side of the story.

# Eagle Cove Beach

🎯 **Local Knowledge** - There is a small cove facing Haro Strait just outside of American Camp that is well worth the short hike. To find Eagle Cove turn right off Cattle Point Rd a few hundred feet before the turn into American Camp. The road sign says **Eagle Cove Drive.** Follow this road about 1/3 mile to a small uneven ten car grassy parking area on your left. There is no sign on the road, at a curve in the road near some trees and heavy underbrush look for a porta-potty and a small park type sign posting usage rules.

The only sign you will find—and it is at the trailhead, not out on the road. This is a residential neighborhood, the parking area is very difficult to spot, the trail down to the beach follows a deep ravine between private properties. If you get to the end of the short drive without finding the trailhead, turn around and look again, it's there!

# Pelindaba Lavender Farm

Excerpt from the internet:

Pelindaba Lavender

*Organic farmers of lavender flowers, distillers of essential oil, and handcrafters of lavender based products for personal care, culinary, aromatherapy, decorative and household uses*

Pelindaba Lavender Farm and Gatehouse Store is at 33 Hawthorne Ln.

This popular inland attraction is conveniently located on a ten mile loop drive, or you can stop by on your way to Lime Kiln on the coast. Unfortunately for cyclists it does require climbing grueling Bailer Hill Rd that I walk part way. You will easily find Hawthorn Ln. by driving along Wold Rd. where you may come across hordes of tourists and acres of flowers. For bicycle riders, Pelindaba Lavendar farm is a great lunch and watering stop with restrooms halfway through the ride.

*Find Wold Rd. on your map, it runs between San Juan Valley Rd. and Bailer Hill Rd.*

## Krystal Acres Alpaca Farm and Country Store

This unique working ranch is a very short distance south of English Camp. (1/2 mile or less) Located at 3501 W Valley Rd.

They welcome visitors and offer a store packed with clothing and accessories made from soft alpaca fleece.

Image courtesy of Krystal Acres Alpaca Farm and Country Store

# English Camp

*I*f you have been to American Camp, you have read and learned all about the *Pig War* so I won't belabor or be redundant. I would like to point out how nice the English had it in comparison. The private land surrounding Garrison Bay and English Camp is studded with expensive homes and exotic ranches, testament to the desirable location.

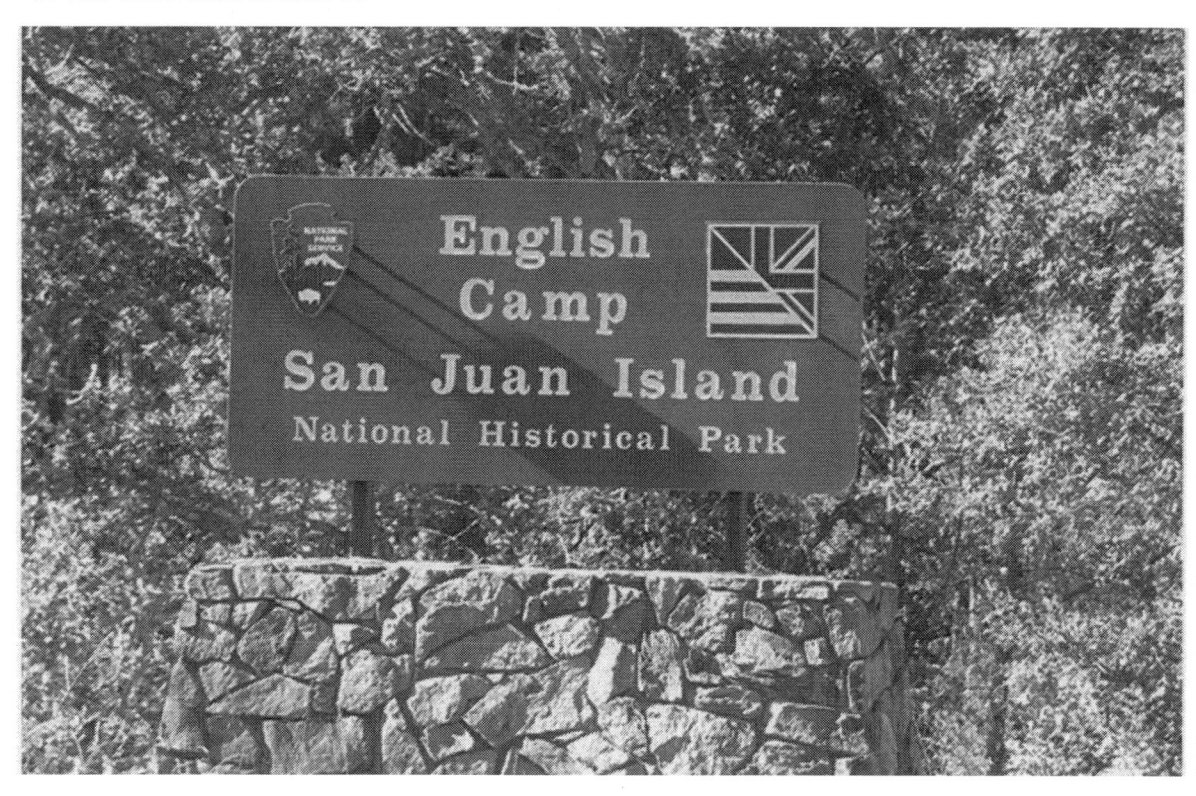

When heading to English Camp, you may as well be planning to visit Roche Harbor since they are close to each other. From Friday Harbor, head up Spring street and turn right on 2nd St, 2nd becomes Guard, turn right on Tucker St, Tucker becomes Roche Harbor Rd. After about 8 miles Turn Left on W Valley Rd, two more miles and you are at the entrance to English camp.

During the twelve-year standoff the English supply vessels docked in front of the garrison and fort, hence naming the tranquil bay, *Garrison Bay*. They undoubtedly used nearby calm Roche Harbor for larger warships and deep draft vessels. Contrast this with the Americans perched on a windswept barren point above the rocks of Haro Strait on one side and after running the sometimes difficult rapids of Cattle Pass, they have a swampy lagoon at the bottom of a long hill on the other side.

Park volunteers use a rebuilt original structure for the interpretive center at English Camp. Plus at the shore edge they have recreated the fort with it's gun ports and 360 degree view. During the summer months volunteers recreate skills and activities highlighting military and pioneer life of the 1860's A traditional English garden with neatly arranged flowers and shrubs was enjoyed by the officers and their wives, and is kept prim and proper by park staff. The grounds consist of an open mowed field with a few large antique trees alongside about a quarter mile of peaceful shore. At the park entrance is a long drive ending at a shaded parking lot with a woodsy trail leading uphill for a semi strenuous hike to the cemetery. Or you might want to spend an hour or so on an easy hiking loop skirting the water. If you decide to hike to the cemetery and then on to the top of 650 foot high Young hill be sure to bring your camera and water bottle.

Formal garden and fort at English Camp. In the distance you can see the dinghy dock and anchored boats. Notice the British flag.

As I said about American Camp, if you visit English Camp, you must also go to American Camp to see the rest of the story.

San Juan Island transit will take you to both. $15 for an all day pass to everywhere.

# For Boaters - Garrison Bay and English Camp

Garrison Bay is easily reachable from Mosquito Pass, the south entrance to Roche Harbor. Long used as a quiet alternative to busy and brassy Roche Harbor, Garrison Bay offers easy anchoring and placid waters. The English Camp park rangers maintain a small dinghy dock for easy access to the park and trails, but you can land your dinghy or kayak anywhere along the open shoreline of the park, even directly under an English Fort and pretend to be sneaking ashore under cover of darkness.

The distance by water from English Camp to Roche Harbor resort is only two miles making it easily a dinghy ride back and forth. By road, it is three miles back to Roche Harbor Resort, just an easy bike ride over mostly level country roads. **Note: Mosquito Pass** current may over power your kicker.

It's possible to bring your big boat into the dinghy dock, but it would be inconsiderate if you hogged all the available footage for very long. Of course dropping off passengers and bicycles and then anchoring to the side, and coming back with the dinghy would be perfectly acceptable and allow you to spend the day exploring the west side of San Juan Island.

# English Camp - Roche Harbor Proximity Map

# San Juan County Park at Smallpox Bay

The only public tenting and RV and hiking/biking campground on San Juan Island is this one.

SJ County Park faces Haro Strait and is on West Side Rd about five miles beyond English Camp, but to get to SJ County Park from Friday Harbor you can take a different road and save a mile or two. Once again head up Spring St. turn right on 2nd, 2nd becomes Guard, Guard becomes Beaverton Valley Rd. Travel about four miles and Beaverton Valley Rd becomes West Valley (the other end of West Valley) follow West Valley about four miles and turn left on Mitchell Bay Rd. After about one and a half miles turn left on West Side Rd. Travel another almost two miles to SJ County Park. There are not any signs pointing the way. The roads and streets have signs, but there aren't any arrows pointing to parks and such.

*Going ashore for a dog walk at Smallpox Bay*

This hilly forested park has a single campsite loop, and a cul-de-sac, all totaling 20 sites, most with ocean views. There is a first come shared hiker/biker/kayaker site with a max. 20 people for $10 each. The park sits on a small bay (Smallpox Bay) with overlooking rocky bluffs. Orca watching is very popular attracting a lot of day use visitors. Some of the campsites will accommodate RV'S twenty feet and under. Reservations are strongly advised for July and August dates. Beginning in March they take reservations at - https://secure.itinio.com/sanjuan/ My daughters have used the reservation system for all the county parks and tell me it works well. The park has running water and flush restrooms but no hook ups.

# Smallpox Bay

$Y$ou can easily bring your big boat into Smallpox Bay and and anchor for the night. The mud and seaweed bottom hooks well with room to swing,  Several boats swinging will be a crowd problem requiring stern ties or placing second anchors.

Being exposed to Haro Strait might bring the swells inside, (see the passing ship?) but this day was  flat until the ships wake arrived.

There are a few easily avoidable charted rocks to one side outside the mouth of the bay.  The county has a sandy looking boat ramp on the beach with no float.  I would advise against using it with anything but 4x4's launching small skiffs and only at higher tides.


Whether by land or sea,  SJ County Park is the perfect answer for orca enthusiasts and kayakers looking for a place to hunker down for the night. The distance by water back to Roche harbor is  about 4 ½ miles  but the distance to Whale Watch Park is less than 2, making this the perfect place to set up camp and maximize your opportunities for sightings.

# Lime Kiln Point Lighthouse and Whale Watch Park

*O*fficially it is *"Lime Kiln Point State Park"* and is claimed to be the best place in the world to see orcas from shore. The sad truth is you may never see one, let alone a pod. Our experience romping around the islands is that we run into sightings unexpectedly, like the photo on the next page. We were not out whale watching, we were on our way to Victoria and got lucky. Another time I was on James Island having my morning coffee staring out over Rosario Strait when a pod of 30,40,50 I lost count – took thirty minutes to go past me. There were so many I thought they might be circling the little island getting counted multiple times. To find Lime Kiln Point State Park, aka Whale Watch Park, you need to keep on the same road past SJ County park another couples miles, or come in on West Side Rd from the other direction. The shortest distance from Friday Harbor to Lime Kiln is about seven and a half miles. Take Spring St. and follow it up the hill and out of town, it becomes San Juan Valley rd, turn left on Douglas Rd. and follow the curve around and you are on Bailer Hill Rd. Bailer Hill Rd. is long, straight and goes up hill, eventually it becomes West Side Rd. and you will get to the park. This is also the way to the Lavender Farm if you turn right onto Wold Rd after climbing over the top of Bailer Hill.

This is a great bike ride - one way or round trip.

The parking lot at Lime Kiln might be full, but people are leaving and arriving constantly. There are restrooms, a short walk takes you to the gift shop and beyond to the lighthouse and interpretive center. The transit stop has a waiting shelter at the parking lot entrance. If you arrive by bicycle and are too tired to have any more fun, just relax and ride the next bus back to town.

For sunset watchers, San Juan Transit runs a sunset bus leaving Friday Harbor 45 minutes before sunset, it takes about an hour and fifteen minutes overall.

This pod of whales traveled between us and an excursion boat offshore at Lime Kiln. We saw them coming from over a half mile. As they got closer the nervous level on our boat steadily rose. The kids were freaking (one was) saying "do something". I had no idea where they were heading except towards us, and I didn't see the need to panic anyway. During the excitement I missed getting some great pictures but I do have some great memories. There were ten to fifteen that we saw probably a lot we missed. The group split and ran down both sides of our 26' foot sailboat. I remember in particular one that was so close I thought that I could jump on to him/her. Wouldn't that have been a picture.

Btw - boaters are supposed to stay away from orcas for their safety. If you find yourself surrounded like we did, you are required to put the transmission in neutral or shut off the motor.

Rocky bluffs and trails along ¼ mile of the shore fronting Lime Kiln Point are dotted with signs and plaques explaining local geology and marine life. Excellent orca watching if the killer whales are around. Excellent picnicking at the scattered tables while you watch and wait.

There are power boater restrictions about getting too close to shore so anchoring and landing a dinghy is out of the question. Most boaters are out about ½ mile, I think that may be the new rule.

Several paths lead to the lighthouse where you can check a reader board for recent sightings. Hopefully that may help you with your own spotting efforts. A naturalist is sometimes on duty answering questions about the local wildlife. Come for a visit, but plan to wait around if you want to see orcas.

# San Juan Islands Sculpture Park

During my first visit to Roche Harbor, I was wandering the grounds and came across this weird looking place on the other side of the road. What caught my attention was how out of place it seemed. Here were some art pieces—great big art pieces out in a field of tall grass. After entering through the fancy iron garden gate, I was soon immersed in the finer side of society, island style—and then a deer jumps out of the grass and snaps me back.

The San Juan Islands Sculpture Park that I discovered is located at 9083 Roche Harbor Rd. It is literally at Roche Harbors front gate. This means when you arrive by boat and rent a slip or anchor and come by dinghy, you can walk up the road or up the lawn and you are there in five minutes. It is very close, so close it would be a real shame if you don't stop by for a visit.

Placed not willy nilly, but thoughtfully on looped paths around their 20 acres of grass and woods are about 150 sculptures from great big whirly gigs down to petite salmon mosaics. In the woods are creatures and things I can't describe. Bongs, gongs and flashy art in motion are in the mix.

Fee admission, but a donation box is present at the entry/exit. They have no employees. I'm told everyone is a volunteer. Some of the art is tagged with the artists name in case a visitor would like to purchase or commission a piece. On more visits than I can remember, I have never seen an attendant, we walk around in silence, sometimes totally alone. It's a very peaceful soothing experience.

I'll wager the deer don't think this is the dinner bell

Being a salty boater, my ignorant first thought is – why isn't it rusty?

50

A black and white still photo does not do this creation justice, it has colored glass, colored metal, and when the wind blows, it comes to life, every component spins or rotates.

51

Some photos are reprinted with permission of the San Juan Islands Sculpture Park
http://sjisculpturepark.com/

Sculpture Park paths with exhibits

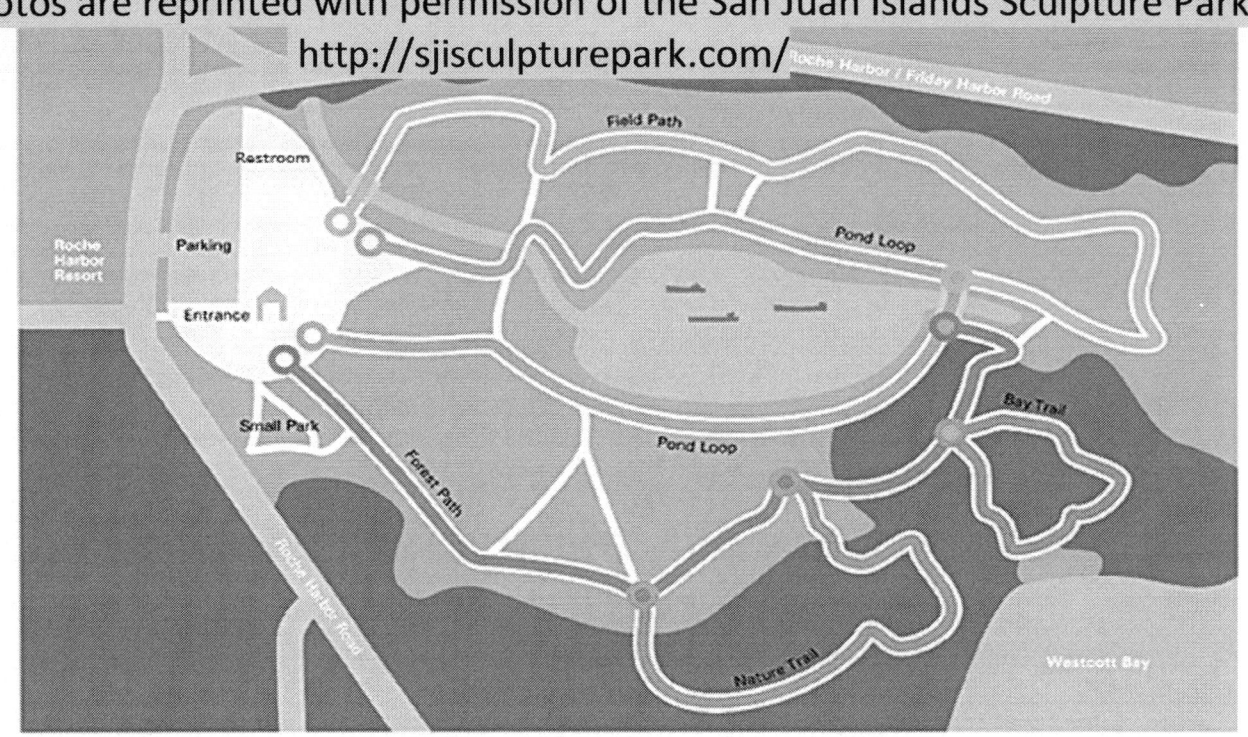

- Pond Loop — 30 min
- Forest Path — 30 min
- Field Path — 20 min
- Nature Trail — 15 min
- Bay Trail — 10 min

We are a 501 c 3 registered non profit. We are funded entirely by donations. Enjoy your visit and thank you for your support.

*Afterglow Vista Mausoleum - missing column - Roche Ha[rbor]*

## Afterglow Vista Mausoleum

My title may not be correct, I have walked to the mausoleum several times, last time I rode my bicycle, but walked it the final portion. It is a cemetery after all, and seemed proper. Some writers name it the Roche Harbor Mausoleum which I'm fairly sure is more descriptive than accurate. It may be best called the "McMillin Mausoleum" since it is their family whose ashes are interred there. In any case it is open to the public, has a story and history worth knowing.

John McMillin owner of the Lime Works used his money and religious philosophy in designing and constructing the tomb. He incorporated symbology for his own satisfaction and to enrich all that would follow long after he was gone.

The missing or broken column in the picture is not a mistake or vandalism, it was his way of symbolizing mans death as breaking his column of life before his work is done. To reach the main level you must walk up steps. The first three steps represent mans three stages in life. The next five steps represent five orders of architecture and mans five senses, the next seven steps represent days of the week and seven liberal arts and sciences. There is more symbology at the mausoleum, you should probably go read it yourself.

Originally planned to have a domed roof, the family later decided to leave it open to the elements letting nature take over.

It is a quiet serenely peaceful place where you will find yourself whispering, and if you visit in the late afternoon you may experience the afterglow as the lowering sun filters golden through the trees.

The walk to the McMillin Mauselum from Roche Harbor, begins at the long dinghy dock at the base of the big lawn next to the swimming pool. I guess I am assuming you came by boat, if you didn't, adjust.

Start walking uphill and to the right so that you don't infringe on any of the rental cabins "open space" Most of us will cut over to the service road and stay off the lawn, in any case, get yourself to the top of the hill. You should be right in front of the Sculpture Garden. Turn left and walk along the road past the end of the airstrip, the road bends left, it's called Afterglow Dr, keep going. You will go past the road to the airport a short distance and then on your right in the woods you will see a trail paralleling the road, maybe even a teensy little sign. Jump on the trail or keep going on the road, after about 500 feet there will be a closed off service type road leading into the trees, and another little sign. Head up the service road or follow the trail and after another 500 feet or so you will find it. My distances are guesses, but this is an easy place to find and you will probably enjoy the experience.

If you are traveling by car, you can park at the service Rd and save walking.

The San Juan Transit van stops at the Sculpture Garden giving you another option.

# Roche Harbor Resort and Marina

As the title above suggests, we might be talking two places. (a place for boats and a cute resort village on shore for people)

I have always said "Roche" (pronouncing as roach) but one day this guy said to me, Roche' with a French accent. I went online to a verbal talking web site, and it is indeed French and sounded like Ruush. I just thought it would interest some of you. I'm sticking with the former.

Writing about Roche Harbor history is outside my comfort level, but I feel it important to learn some to truly appreciate this place. The following article, hits some good points, so I am reprinting an excerpt.

I found this article at https://www.sos.wa.gov/legacy/cities_detail.aspx?i=25

## The History of Roche Harbor Village
### Formerly the Roche Harbor Lime & Cement Company

This information is provided courtesy of Deborah Hopkins, Marketing Director of Roche Harbor Village. All photos are provided by Roche Harbor Village.

The story of Roche Harbor began nearly 200 years ago in 1787 when Captain de Haro and his crew became the first Europeans to sail among the forested San Juan Islands. The Haro Strait, which divides the United States from Vancouver Island, derives its name from this Spanish explorer.

In 1845, four years before the California Gold Rush, the Hudson's Bay Company posted a notice of possession on San Juan Island and built a log trading post at the head of Roche Harbor on the northwest shoulder of the island. The British traders and settlers were not the only people interested in the San Juan Islands; American settlers moving west were also in search of land.

By 1857, three years before Civil War, both the United States and Britain were claiming the San Juan Islands and a dispute arose over the western end of the boundary between British and American territory. The dispute lay dormant during the Civil War, but by 1871 the United States and Great Britain selected Germany's Kaiser Wilhelm to arbitrate the dispute. In 1872 Wilhelm awarded possession of the San Juan Islands to the United States.

During the dispute, known as the "Pig War," and joint occupancy by both American and British soldiers, lime deposits were discovered along the ridge above the harbor. In predictable military fashion, Lieutenant Roche, commander of the Royal Marines, and in whose honor the harbor was named, sought to keep his garrison troops busy by having them quarry and burn the limestone. Lime was a major necessity in the production of steel, plaster, cement and paper, and was shipped worldwide from Roche Harbor.

After the war ended peacefully, and a few days after the British withdrawal, a man named Joe Ruff took out a pre-emption claim on the land around Roche Harbor, but did nothing with it in the way of extracting lime. In 1881 two brothers, Robert and Richard Scurr, bought Roche Harbor and started the islands' lime industry. There was no town at Roche Harbor until John S. McMillin, a Tacoma lawyer, discovered the richest and largest deposit of lime in the Northwest and began negotiations for their claims and property in 1884. By 1886 the Tacoma and Roche Harbor Lime Company was incorporated and becoming a large-scale American business.

McMillin built the 20-room Hotel de Haro in 1886 around the original Hudson's Bay Post. By 1890 a company town had grown up around the magnificent hotel. It consisted of a completely modern lime factory, a barrel works, warehouse, docks, ships, piers, offices, company store, church, school, barns and homes. The homes were for both the owner and workers, all neatly painted and kept in good condition as property of the company.

At its peak, Roche Harbor boasted about 800 residents with single men being barracked in large bunkhouses along the hillside beside the church and families housed in the rows of one and two-story cottages lining the slope from schoolhouse to the beach. The town was completely independent with autonomous power, water and telephone systems. The workers at Roche Harbor were paid in scrip -- good only at the company store and was still in use when the town was sold in 1956 -- but they could draw their wages in currency when they desired.

In 1956 Reuben J. Tarte, a Seattle businessman, purchased all 4,000 acres of Roche Harbor which included 12 miles of coastline. Tarte and his family set about restoring the hotel and warehouse, scouring the site for scattered hotel furniture and remnants. Roche Harbor then became a resort for boating families. Tarte's son Neil Tarte and his wife, Margaret, continued running the hotel and marina after Reuben's death, the area has since become a popular place for boaters and vacationers.

4th of July at Roche Harbor is loads of fun, but try to arrive on the 3rd to get a good spot.

Once you arrive by boat, plane, shuttle, car or on bicycle and mix in with the others strolling the grounds and docks you will quickly become immersed in the small village atmosphere. This is intentional, the resort planned many years ago to refine and promote the comfortable village feeling. I think they succeeded. When you first arrive you will be drawn to the carts and booths set up *"Main Street Saturday Market Style"* in front of the *Company Store*. My favorite is the ice cream shop.

Guests are encouraged to participate in everything from strolling the manicured gardens to hiking trails, orca watching excursions, to sea kayak rentals. The large heated swimming pool is a hit for the young at heart and their kids too.

Boaters that are sometimes 2-3 weeks from their home port depend on the store being stocked with anything and everything and it is.

When you are a mile out, call the harbormaster on 78A for slip assignment or for complimentary tie-up while you shop. They have over 350 slips and handle 150' yachts, 30 and 50 amp service and water is at the slips. To find the fuel and ice simply point your vessel up the fairway leading towards the fluttering flags out on the end of the wharf.  Your crew can run up the steps to the store while you fuel.  It's that easy! (see the section just for boaters)

They have three restaurants to choose from, McMillin's, featuring fresh, local cuisine. The Madrona Bar and Grill, and my favorite breakfast stop in the San Juans—Lime Kiln Café. It's at the top of the gangway, directly above the dinghy dock overlooking the marina.

Each 4th of July travelers and especially boaters arrive from everywhere for celebration activities.  My favorite besides the bang up fireworks barge display is the blind dinghy race where the person rowing is blindfolded and taking directions from a helper yelling left, left, faster, right, no your other right.  Of course it is a wild splashing melee.

🎯 Tip     Something that is very special and dear to many is the colors ceremony, more well known as retiring the flag.  Just before sunset each night during the summer, members of the Roche Harbor staff form a color guard out on the lawn overlooking the marina. They march to the flagpoles and lower the British, Canadian, Washington, and Roche Harbor flags to piped in songs on the public address system. Then before lowering the last flag a loud cannon booms across the night, white smoke pours out the guns bore while the color guard lowers and folds the American flag.

After the echoes stop and the flag is down an announcer tells the news of the day, weather updates, special occasion announcements and personal announcements such as wedding, birthdays, anniversary, etc.

🎯 Tip if you have a special message that you want to surprise someone with, this is your chance to be romantic or at least surprisingly thoughtful. All you have to do is go to the front desk inside the Hotel De Haro to make arrangements for them to announce your personal message. In the afternoon before the flag ceremony, make your request. I suggest that you write everything down on paper so nothing is missing, names, dates, birthday, proposal, get it all down so all the announcer needs to do is read it. Don't mess up this opportunity to make a special moment perfect. (Or embarrass your teenager).

## For Boaters Going to Roche Harbor

*A* few thoughts for new visitors anticipating anchoring in Roche Harbor.

The vast majority of watercraft making their way to Roche Harbor for the first time will be coming from Anacortes or Bellingham or points south. I make this bold statement because that's the direction the mainland lies, so once inside the San Juan's you will be coming through Spieden Channel, and then turn into Roche Harbor.

First off, you need to decide which side of little Pearl Island to transit. After carefully scrutinizing the chart plotter and watching other boaters you will learn that skippers use both sides. I use both sides myself because I am like most skippers and I take the shortest route depending on where I'm coming from or going to. That being said, the west side of Pearl Island is the side the biggest yachts use, or the ones coming from Canada or off Haro Strait. The east side of Pearl gets down to one fathom at low tides and has some splotches of seaweed that always make me wary until I locate and get past them. When I travel the east side I pay very close attention to my depth sounder, hold my speed down, and watch the looming sea floor next to me. When I come in on the west side of Pearl, I just drive up the middle thinking about finding my anchoring handling gloves, or what's for dinner.

Once inside, the enormity of Roche Harbor hits you; the place is big and always has boats going to and fro, so watch your converging courses so that at least one of you will turn away if needed. You can anchor anywhere your heart desires, but use some common sense. Natural thoroughfares develop as the anchorage fills up, for instance the passage where you just arrived will have more boats heading for the docks. You probably shouldn't anchor in front of them or even nearby to the side unless you want to be rocked by wakes all night. On the far side of the bay boats will be coming from Mosquito Pass. Same thing, they will follow the shortest course to the Roche docks and few watch their wakes. You may want to anchor more in the middle where it may be peaceful.

The entire bay is thirty to forty feet deep pretty much everywhere out in the middle and in front of the marina. That means if you only brought with you an anchor and one hundred feet of rode, you won't have enough scope for anything but benign zero wind conditions. I suggest you bring another hundred feet to be safe and secure while sleeping.

Another major consideration when choosing where to anchor is your tender ride to the dinghy dock. The time and effort rowing or motoring is a big deal for me, and I'll bet the mates will agree. The times we have anchored with only a few hundred feet to paddle has allowed us to immerse ourselves into the village ambience. Being able to run to the store (or bathroom) in mere minutes makes a big difference. Turning kids loose in a kayak or dinghy and watching them the entire way to shore is big in our book too.

My favorite place to anchor at Roche Harbor is not out in the bay, it's on the left side clear in by the marina. That's left side as you face shore from out in the middle. You can run your boat in very close opposite the transient boat slips but stay near shore, so you don't block traffic. The water gets a little thin but you can anchor within yelling distance of the long dinghy dock below the swimming pool. During the three day Fourth of July experience, power and sail boaters will raft along this side strip creating a solid barrier. We almost always place the big hook out front and run a floating yellow line out back to hook a grapple anchor in the rocky shallows stretching our boat in the middle. On busy weekends there may be twenty boats, many rafting, doing this.

Don't bother attempting to anchor on the other side of the marina, that's the right side as you face the marina from out in the bay. The right side is either too shallow or you will be too close to the docks for good manners. We spent an hour trying to anchor on the right side before giving up. Don't forget, it's not smart to park your car on a freeway or anchor your boat in a thoroughfare or fairway.

One last thing I would like to pass along, you should know that *Kenmore Air* lands their seaplanes many times each day adding to the fun. I once counted seven planes taxiing on the water or at the dock at the same time. They seem to favor the west side of Pearl Island for their approach. Yet another reason not to anchor in a thoroughfare.

**Slip assignments:**

When you come to stay in a slip, you will need to call the Harbormaster for a slip assignment. There is no breakwater like at Friday Harbor, all the lineal dock space on the outside is reserved for one thing or another. The red floats outside the Customs shack are only to be used for business with customs. Down from customs is a spot for airplanes. Some hundred foot yachts have prior dibs on the rest.

When you near Roche Harbor call on channel 78A, if you are just getting ice cream and ice, they may tell to take the empty hundred foot spot anyway, but it is best that you let them be in charge.

Once you get a slip assignment for the evening, ask the person on the radio for directions, they may ask you what your boat looks like to make visual contact and direct you. Tell them if you need assistance docking, sometimes the wind will come up blowing you sideways. They have lots of staff and will meet you at your slip.

Roche's slips were intimidating the first time we tied up there. The float was much higher than we were accustomed to and the cleats were these huge timber things. We felt small (we were) and not wealthy (true too) and the surrounding yachties were all dressed to the nines. Linda still talks about it.

Don't worry about registering or paying the rent, someone will come around later and get you all set up. Just get tied up, plugged in and relax. As a guest of Roche Harbor, you may use the pool and all the amenities just like you came by car or plane and were staying in the hotel.

## Dinghy Docks at Roche Harbor

I have already told you that on the left side over by the lawn and swimming pool is a long long pier that extends into deep water. This dock by far holds more tenders than the others, except at low tide half the dock is in the mud, oops. And it is a little bit of a walk over to the store and restrooms. There are two ways to get to the other dinghy dock. You may continue the way you are headed past the long pier towards the store; you will then pass between pilings and ghost slowly under the overhead wharf to tie up on the much underused back side of the dinghy dock. Or you may run all the way around the first row of floats (the main guest dock) probably where your slip assignment is, and paddle or motor towards the fuel dock beneath the flags. Go past the fuel dock until you can't go any further and you will be on the other side of the previous described location. Just steps away are the stairway to the restrooms, store, and Lime Kiln Café. By the way, there are individual restrooms with showers on the other side of the building; you don't have to put up with the community style facilities.

The top image on the opposite page is of the newish dinghy dock, so new in fact that it was not included in the Roche Harbor marina and grounds map on page 64. When you study the Roche Harbor marina map, look for Shipwreck Beach just above the pool and tennis court – that is where the dinghy dock is found.

At low tide we still had enough depth to tie up crossways out on the end and load up bicycles.

As I said and the picture attests - the dinghy dock is challenging at low water. Look on the right side of the picture, that row of boats is where I anchor and then it's a short paddle to the dock.

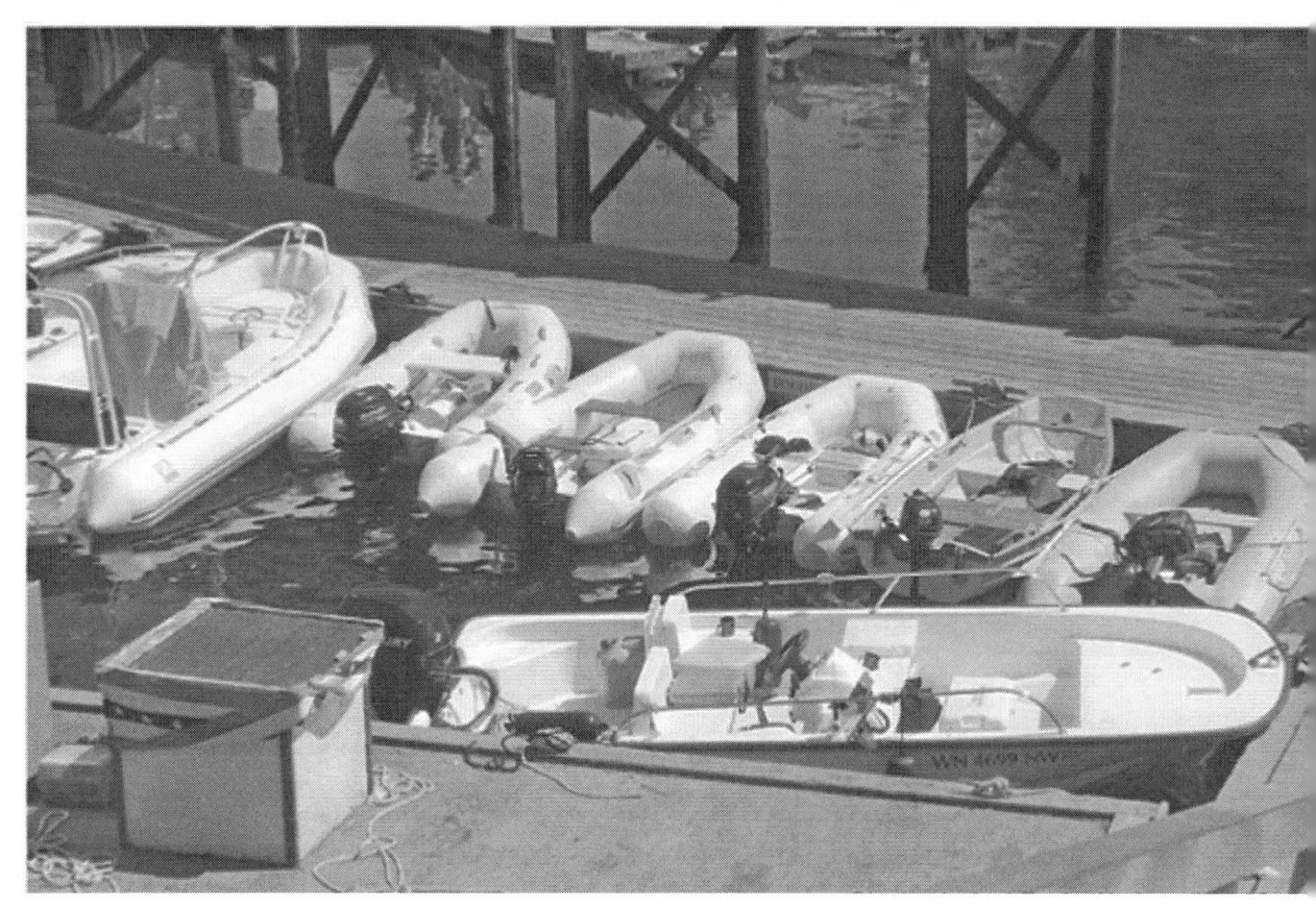

Go past the fuel dock to get here but it's full, the other side is empty. To get there, go past the lawn and long dinghy dock, under the wharf and between the pilings.

# Roche Harbor

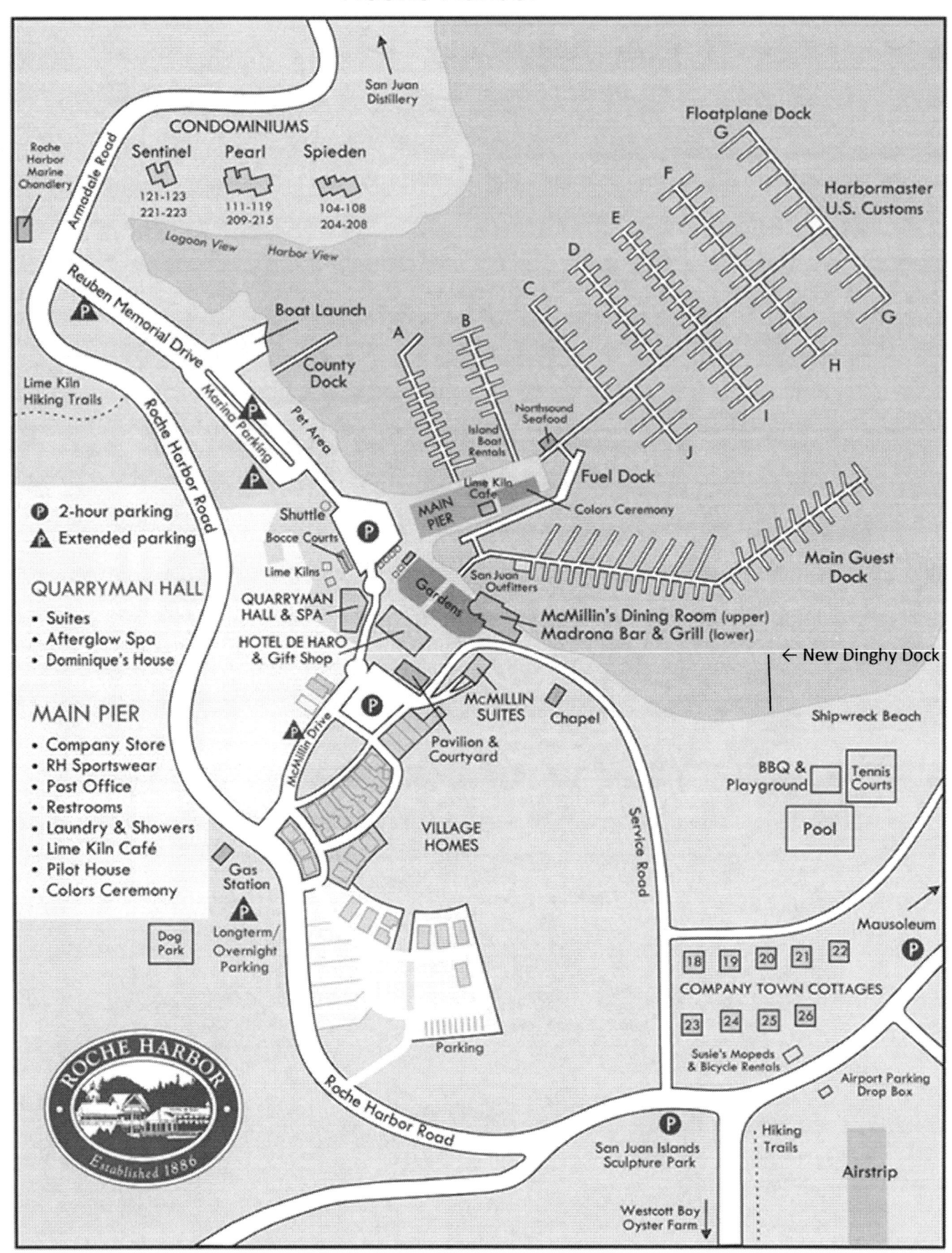

# Lakedale Resort at Three Lakes

*T*here are only two places where you can pitch tents on San Juan Island. #1 San Juan County Park at Smallpox Bay on the west shore, or #2 Lakedale Resort, which is inland on private lakes.

Surfing the Lakedale Resort web site, I was able to determine they offer over 40 tent sites, costing $50 and up per nt. RV sites, cabins, canvas cabins, and hiker biker camps at $40 per night. They offer quite a bit more traveler/tourist/vacationer amenities.

The resort is about 4 ½ miles outside Friday Harbor on the road to Roche Harbor. Lakedale Resort is a regular stop for San Juan Transit, so as a guest you can park your car and still tour the islands sights.

Leave your kayak on the car – to protect native fish species they don't allow outside watercraft but you may rent their boats.

Due to such limited camping facilities on San Juan Island, and some being shut down in the off season, I don't recommend coming to the San Juan's without a plan where to stay. Reservations are the answer.
>> http://www.lakedale.com/map/

Lakedale Resort: 4313 Roche Harbor Rd, Friday Harbor, WA 98250 - 360-378-2350

*True or false? "There are no traffic lights in the San Juan's"*
Hint, the answer is not in this book

# Rueben Tarte Memorial Park

Rueben Tarte Park is a day use county park on the shore of San Juan Channel. Like most day use parks the facilities are minimal providing primarily a legal beach access and not much more. At Tarte Park the entrance drive dives down a steep hill to a turn around, but you are supposed to park at the top of the hill and walk down. It is a healthy walk down and that alone discourages many including me.

You can expect to be alone but no guarantees, at the bottom of the hill is a small eroded point jutting out from shore creating two miniature beaches covered in pebbles and winter driftwood.

You might approach from seaward but it willl be tough spotting the park without gps or some help. The little coves offer no anchoring protection and there is really no reason to go ashore anyway. On the other hand if you are in your car and crave a close to town hideaway where you can commune with shore life in relative peace and quiet, this is the perfect place for you.

From town take Roche Harbor Dr past Lakedale Resort about three miles, turn right on Rouleau Rd, turn right on Limestone Point Rd, right on San Juan Dr. The park will be on your left in a woodsy pull over.
Latitude: 48.61264 |
Longitude: 123.09775
gps coordinates are for kayakers or boaters

# Stuart Island
## Reid Harbor - Prevost Harbor - Turn Point Lighthouse

The San Juans hold the distinction of being the NW corner of Washington. Stuart Island is the NW corner of the San Juans. There is a plaque on the ocean side of the lighthouse that marks the boundary - well I'll just let you read it yourself, see the image below.

**TURN POINT REFERENCE MARK**
TURNING POINT 4 OF THE UNITED STATES AND CANADIAN BOUNDARY BETWEEN THE 49TH PARALLEL AND THE PACIFIC OCEAN IS 2316.5 METERS N 75°33'9" W OF THIS MONUMENT. (NORTH AMERICAN DATUM OF 1927)

*T*his means the corner boundary of the United States is 2316 ½ meters (1.4 miles) west (in the water) of this bronze plaque.   (I think it is about 1750 feet deep out there)

The point off the tip of Stuart Island is commonly know as Turn Point, and the lighthouse is Turn Point Lighthouse. Ships heading to and from Vancouver Canada must turn here so the name is appropriate for sure. The lighthouse, like all of them, is automated now. The keepers and their families are remembered in photos and sometimes heroic deeds recorded in history. Today, volunteers man the refurbished lighthouse and station buildings allowing visitors to tour inside. Photos and news clippings of the early keepers cover the walls and fill notebooks and albums enough to captivate buffs for hours.

If you are interested in watching orcas, Turn Point may be your best bet, very definitely exceeding Whale Watch Park for up close viewing. Just like the ships that must turn, feeding orcas chasing salmon do the same thing except the orcas swim very close to shore and the elevated cliff gives you a great downward angle. Inside the building are orca photos taken by volunteers.

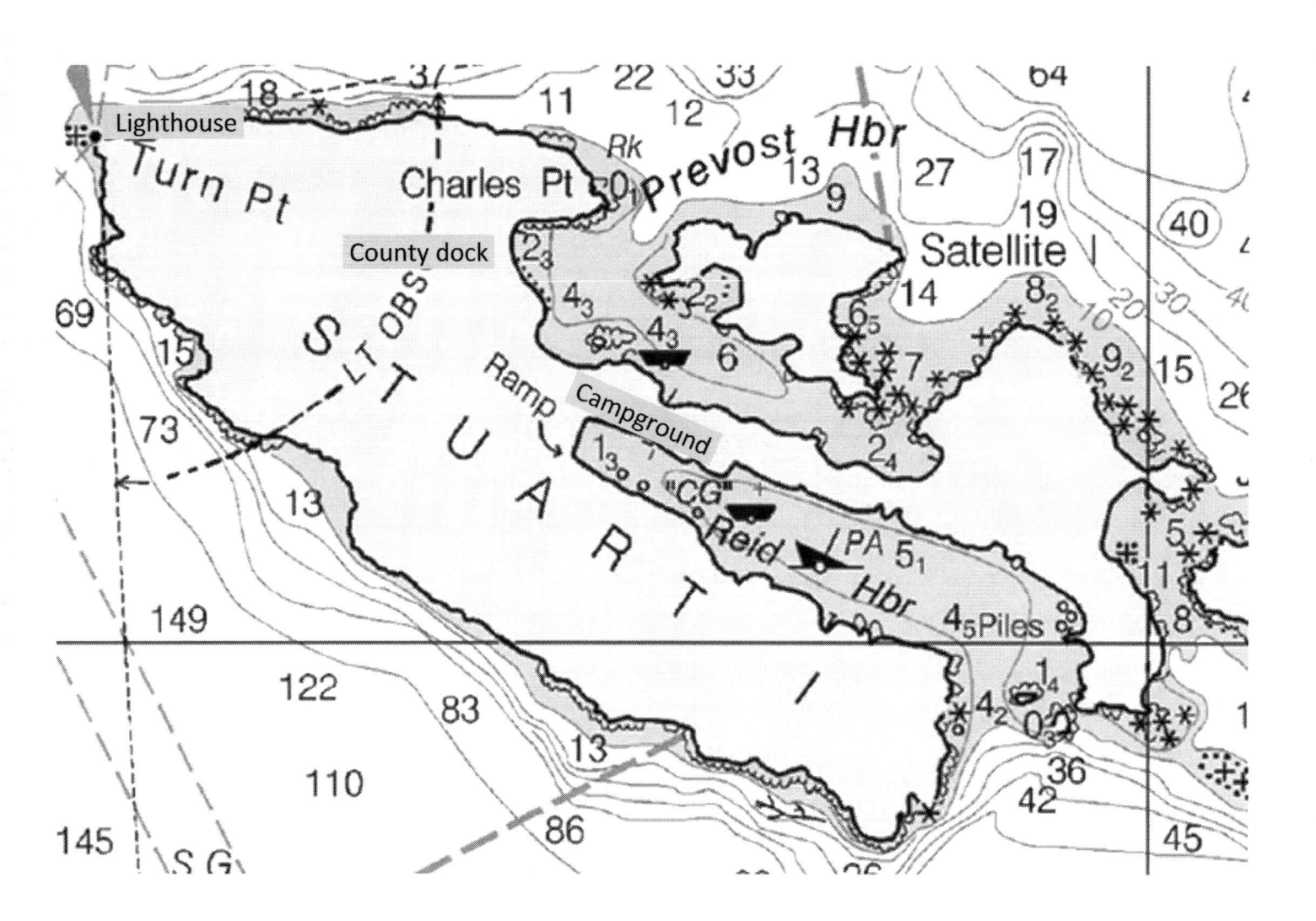

Sometime around 1874 after the Pig War settled ownership of the islands, our government partialed out chunks of Stuart Island and gave them to early pioneers to homestead, consequently almost the entire island is privately held and development is minimal. They no longer support a school and only a few call themselves full time residents. Stuart Island State Park comprises 85 acres which isn't much, but it has over six miles of shoreline on two large bays. I can't describe Stuart as a dog bone shape like Jones and James Island, but I will describe it as a finger island similar to Sucia. The fingers being the long bays separated by a skinny strip of land. At this very narrow and low isthmus, the State has built two docks, one on each side. On the east is Prevost Harbor, the west is Reid Harbor. The Prevost side has a 128 foot dock, the Reid side has 96 feet, both docks are useable all year and have plenty of depth. In between the docks on shore is a small campground.

**Prevost wharf and float**

At the head of Reid Harbor where it shallows into a marshy area is a popular kayaker campground. Both campgrounds are typical with fire pits picnic tables and rustic toilets. Drinking water is piped in, and you must pack out all your trash at all outer island parks.

**Reid Harbor float**

**Trail to Turn Point Lighthouse**

*T*his hike is one excellent reason for coming to Stuart Island for a day trip or overnight. The road portion of this hike begins essentially at the kayaker campground, but you probably can't or don't want to take your boat in there. Dinghy maybe, but not me.

Start out leaving your dinghy at one of the two docks, and then make your way to the Reid side of the isthmus, look for an obvious trail with a sign. It will go uphill at first skirting the bluff with peek-a-boo's of your boat anchored in Reid Harbor. Did you bring your camera? Better go back and get it. After a relatively short jaunt the trail nosedives down an endless string of stairs bringing you to the kayaker campground at the head of the bay. After going around the campground the trail comes out on the gravel road and you begin a long arduous yet gentle and shaded uphill walk. Keep an eye out for a swing in a tree on the right side, but don't give up as I know some do. At the top of the hill is the closed, newer one room school house and a museum of sorts in the older one room schoolhouse. **Continued pg 72**

## Boundary Pass Traders

For as many years as I have been visiting there has been a family business on Stuart Island calling themselves Boundary Pass Traders. They screen print T-shirts and sell them to visiting boaters. They have set up what can best be described as a self-help do-it-yourself kiosk in the woods beside the road just before the schoolhouse. These are very professional screen prints featuring San Juan Islands themes, ie orcas, pirates, and cute sayings. What is unique is their honor system, there is no one there, you simply pick out what you like and take it home, they include an envelope for you to mail them payment later. They keep the inventory neatly bagged in a large pirate chest and have samples hanging from lines in the trees.

Did I mention they set out a cooler full of ice water and paper cups? After walking up the hill you will be glad to have a drink.

## Continued from Trail to the Lighthouse

Get some needed rest while you are looking over the school museum (self guided) and picking out t-shirts, but then keep on trucklin down the road. It's now easy walking but you still have almost 1 ½ miles to the lighthouse. About ¾ mile further, you will turn left on the road that comes up from the county dock, there is another water cooler and another pirate chest full of shirts for the hikers coming from the county dock direction. More about the county dock a little later.

By now you will have most likely passed other hikers on their way back saying things like, "not much further," and "we saw some orcas," (meaning you won't).

When you first get to the light stations buildings, look for a brown fiberglass restroom on the right. Lighthouse volunteers have traditionally decorated the privy's inside, take a peek. Flowers, perfumes, carpet, artwork all are unexpected yet oddly very nice.

Plan to spend some time out on this picturesque point. There is lots of history and if you are lucky some orcas will entertain you. The walk back is not as hard, but it is still about 2 ½ miles back to the boat. Sometimes I think of the islands few school children that walked the stairs and hill everyday, and some came by rowboat in the rain. If I remember the history lesson correctly, the last class had only a few students. The school closed in 2013.

## Stuart Island County Dock

As a much shorter alternative, to the hike just described, we now take our bicycles, and start out at the county dock.

At the far north end of Prevost Harbor is the county wharf and float for dinghy's and the mail boat. You can't miss it, it's the only one. We pull in and unload bikes, gear and people and then I anchor fifty feet away coming back in the dinghy. Pedaling up the gradual incline to the road coming from the school and Reid harbor is fairly easy, but we still stop at the Boundary Trader pirate chest on the corner for a cool drink and then push on.

**TIP** About a quarter mile before you get to the lighthouse the road suddenly drops down a steep hill, so steep that we have fallen trying to keep our bikes under control, forcing us to walk. Of course, because of the steepness, we can't ride back up either. We now padlock our bikes to each other and leave them at the top, walking the last little bit. Locking the bikes seems untrusting, but losing them would seriously impact our great attitude so I lock them. You should have no trouble spotting where to park and walk, its where you panic seconds before crashing.

## Kayaking and Small Boats from Roche Harbor to Reid Harbor

Of course you can paddle just about anywhere in the San Juans, but the shorter hops are preferred The distance from Roche to Reid Harbor is under three miles making the trip a popular kayak camping trip. With a suitable weather and calm sea's forecast, and timing the current a, paddler can make the trip in about an hour, in fact riding the current both ways is completely doable.

# Jones Island

*I* love Jones Island, and so does my family and everyone I have ever talked with that has been there. That declaration ought to sum it up but I guess you deserve some facts.

The entire island is a Marine State Park. It's a dog bone Island meaning it has two ends with two bays separated by an isthmus. Jones is about 2 miles west and around the corner from Deer Harbor and roughly ½ mile offshore from Orcas Island. Technically, it is in San Juan Channel. Friday Harbor and Roche Harbor are both about 5 miles away, making Jones very convenient for slow boaters, kayakers, day trippers you name it, all are likely to be found kicking back at Jones.

*I don't recommend this stunt, at the time it seemed ok. I count eight masts in the cove.*

The North Cove has a new hundred feet plus dock holding three to five boats on each side depending on lengths. Out in the bay at last count was 4 anchor buoys, and there is lots of room for anchoring. The beach is small pebbles with a very dinghy friendly slope. It's easy to land an inflatable or small dinghy without getting your feet wet. You can anchor 75 feet out in deep water. The thousand feet long crescent shaped beach is topped with a low to medium bank and waterfront campsites. All total between north and south coves, Jones has about two dozen campsites with fire pits. Fresh water from a well is piped to both coves. Jones is outfitted with standard composting toilets that are quite nice. Well nice compared to some that are not nice at all.

South Cove does not have a dock but does have a couple anchor buoys. The south cove has a large meadow with apple trees and Adirondack shelters that may be reserved. Group camp areas may be reserved in both coves.   You may reserve your campsite here > http://parks.state.wa.us/525/Jones-Island

The island has several easy to hike loops that follow the shore for excellent views and casual walks.

The black tail deer on Jones are legendary for their tameness and small size. I have had deer meet me at the water when I dinghy ashore and try to steal my dinner around campfires. Once a little four-point buck came up to my son for noggin rubs. You should know that it is illegal to feed the deer and makes you subject to criticism and eviction from the park. I've always suspected they have fleas too.

Jones Island is a place you will not want to leave and draws you back, count on it.

*Jones Island north cove float at high tide*

Note: Since this picture was taken they have replaced the float and pilings with galvanized.

Kayak Tip: Come to Jones if you are a kayaker looking for an easy protected paddle and a great place to camp. Be sure to read the kayak chapter with suggested trips.

Hiking Jones island is easy. There are several loop trails that circle and cut across the island. The shoreline trails follow the contour giving peeks and photo ops of San Juan Channel vessel traffic. Even though deer frequent the campground areas, you may expect to come across others bedded down on your hikes. Otters and raccoons live everywhere in the San Juans including Jones. They will climb on your boat and tear apart anything left out, leaving cute little footprints behind as proof. They can lift lids on coolers – you have been warned.

This fellow looks cute until he trashes your decks and poops on your coiled dock lines.

Is she invisible or tame? It's easy to enjoy Jones Island

76

North cove at Jones - that's Turtleback Mountain on Orcas in the background

Kids seem to always find each other around tide pools next to the gangway at Jones

All of Jones Island is your personal park to enjoy, there is no private land or structures except a pump house and water tank back in the woods.

According to the Washington Parks web site Jones Island is 188 acres and 25,000 feet of shoreline. The numbers mean little to most of us. For perspective, just the shoreline trails take about two hours to complete, including breaks and photo stops. You may take short morning coffee walks as small as fifteen minutes or as long as you like.

### Hazard warning

**First rock!** - as you approach the north cove of Jones, **be sure to locate on your chart** a submerging reef. It is very close to the cove entrance just off the east side. At high tide all you see is a post. But never depend on those things, one day the post will be missing. Further out is a buoy, to be safe if you are unsure, go around the buoy.

**Second rock!** - about a quarter mile east of the above spot is another awash reef. Both these reefs are exactly where you might be coasting along looking at seals and day dreaming. My advice is the same for all shallow water operation. #1 find it on your chart and then visually spot the problem before you crunch, or #2 stay farther off shore in deep water. Not much can ruin your outing more than running aground five minutes from your destination.

See rocks marked below!

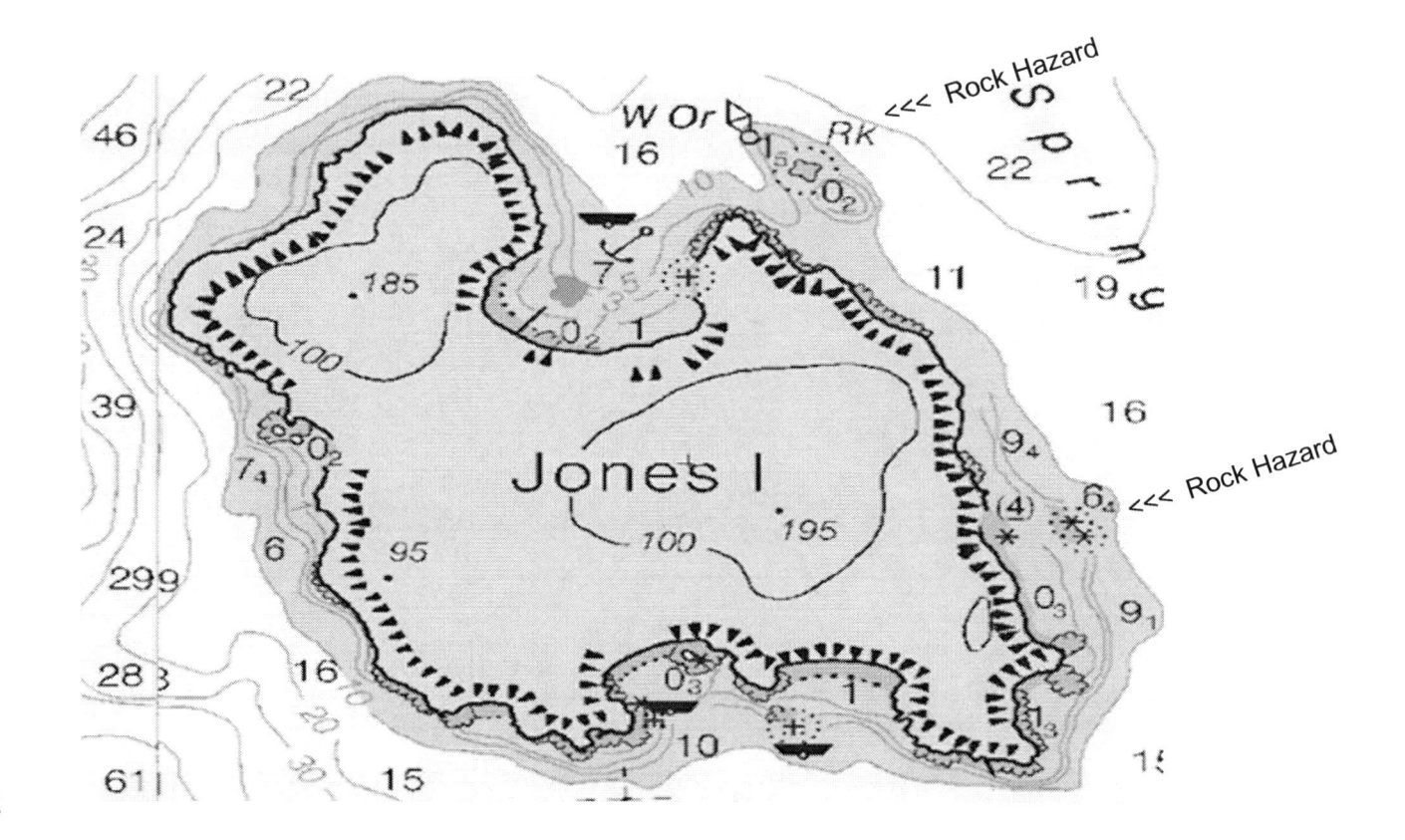

# Orcas Island Quick Check

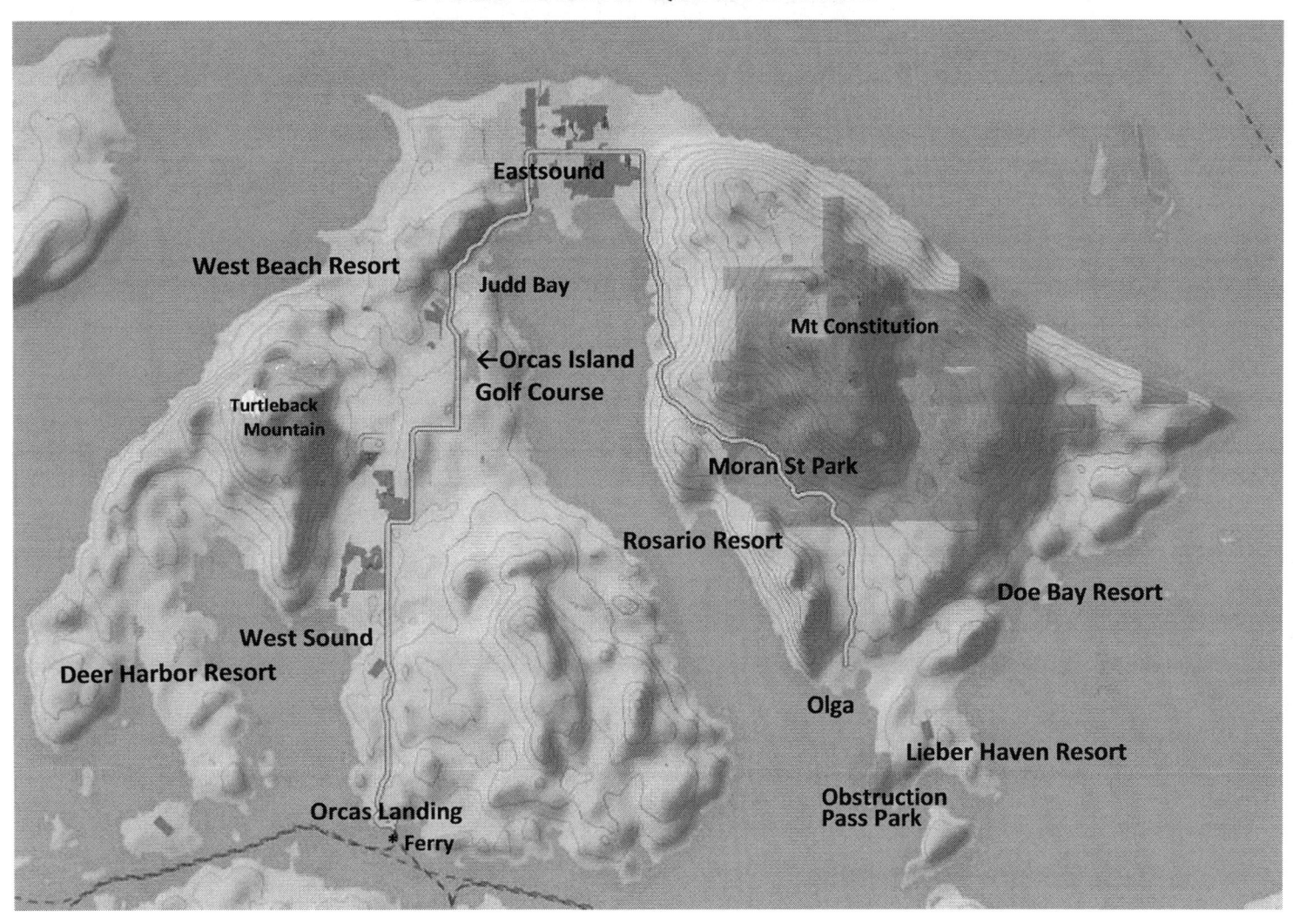

*Map of Orcas Island showing locations: Eastsound, West Beach Resort, Judd Bay, Orcas Island Golf Course, Turtleback Mountain, Mt Constitution, Moran St Park, Rosario Resort, Doe Bay Resort, West Sound, Deer Harbor Resort, Olga, Lieber Haven Resort, Orcas Landing Ferry, Obstruction Pass Park.*

**Camping:**
- Moran State Park
- Obstruction Pass State Park
- West Beach Resort
- Doe Bay Resort

**Marinas & Docks:**
- Deer Harbor
- West Sound
- West Beach Resort
- Olga
- Rosario Resort
- Eastsound
- Orcas Landing
- Lieber Haven Resort

**Safe Anchorages:**
- Olga (Buck Bay)
- Deer Harbor
- Judd Bay
- Rosario (Cascade Bay)
- West Beach Resort
- Doe Island

**Activities:**
- Farmers Market, every Sat. in Eastsound (early May to late Sept.)
- Music festivals in Eastsound on the Village Green
- Kayak and/or bicycle rentals
    - Eastsound
    - Deer Harbor
    - Lieber Haven Resort
- Doe Bay Resort
- Orcas Landing (ferry terminal)
- Outer Island Expeditions

- Golf - Orcas Island Country Golf Course

- Whale Watching - Fishing
    - Outer Island Expeditions
    - Deer Harbor Charters
    - Orcas Island Eclipse Charters

79

# Orcas Island Transit Stops

Orcas ferry landing – West Sound – Turtleback Mtn. Trailhead - Deer Harbor – Golf Course – Eastsound Market – Rosario Resort – Moran ST Park –

**The Transit runs on Orcas Island  Fri - Sat - Sun only - from June thru Sept.**
See scheduled p/u times here → http://www.sanjuantransit.com/Orcas%202016.pdf

*I* think Orcas Island has the most name recognition of all the San Juans. The  distinctive horseshoe shape makes it easy for me to spot it on maps and charts.  It just barely beats out San Juan Island for biggest island.

Being one of the big four Islands it has ferry service to appropriately named Orcas Landing.  Orcas landing (now a village) is exactly that, a place to land the ferry for loading and unloading.  Of course there are a couple places to eat and the requisite tourist type souvenir stores, but for the most part people get off the ferry and drive away.  I suggest that you drive a quarter block and pull into a shop or parking lot and let the line of  tailgating cars leave you behind - its time to slow down and enjoy yourself.

Bicycles are first on and first off, the majority are bicycle campers, a growing segment of traveler in the San Juans.   Inter-island ferry service is free to foot and bicycle passengers. Expect no wait lines, no checking on or off, just walk on and go.   (Kayaks require a small freight fee of around $10 )

🎯 Kayak tip - bigger boaters too: Orcas Village landing is a public float right next to the ferry terminal. You may launch your kayaks that you lugged over on the ferry. There is also a long term parking lot if you brought your car along. This is probably the easiest and cheapest way to go kayaking and camping in the San Juans. (Hint - head for Jones Island) Boaters out and about should know that the float is day use only and open to battering wakes. Try to tie up on the inside.

You can see in this image, private boats at Orcas Landing, in the distance are kayaks that just left.

## West Sound

West Sound is the small community at the top of West Sound, the water body. A lot of people simply drive through on their way to Deer Harbor. They have some bed and breakfast Inns and a cafe. There is a well outfitted private marina that offers fuel, pump out, haul out, and repairs. Overnight dock space for transient boaters is available. They cater mostly to locals for year around business.

*Did you know that the San Juans have half the rain that Seattle has?*

# Turtleback Mountain

You may ride the transit bus, drive your car or bicycle to Turtleback Mountain. It's up to you to do the hiking once you get to the parking lot. The parking lot and south trailhead are on the road to Deer Harbor, about *seven miles* from Orcas Landing. Look for a right turn off Deer Harbor Rd onto Wild Rose Ln., *one mile* after you pass Crow Valley Rd. The marked parking lot and trail is just a short way up Wild Rose Ln.

There are several loop hikes in the 1700 acre preserve leading to overlooks and vistas of the San Juans. Expect to have quiet solitude while you commune with nature on your three mile round trip.

## SAN JUAN COUNTY LAND BANK

### TURTLEBACK MOUNTAIN PRESERVE

Turtleback Mountain Preserve has been protected through the efforts of the San Juan County Land Bank, the San Juan Preservation Trust, the Trust for Public Land, and more than 1,500 private donors. Turtleback's 1,718 acres provide essential habitat for a diversity of native plants and wildlife. Over 8 miles of trail meander through quiet forests, grasslands, and rare Garry oak woodlands.

- Stay on designated trails
- Leash your dogs and pack out waste
- Daytime and non-motorized use only
- No hunting, camping or fires
- Take nothing and leave nothing

For information call 360.378.4402 or visit www.sjclandbank.org

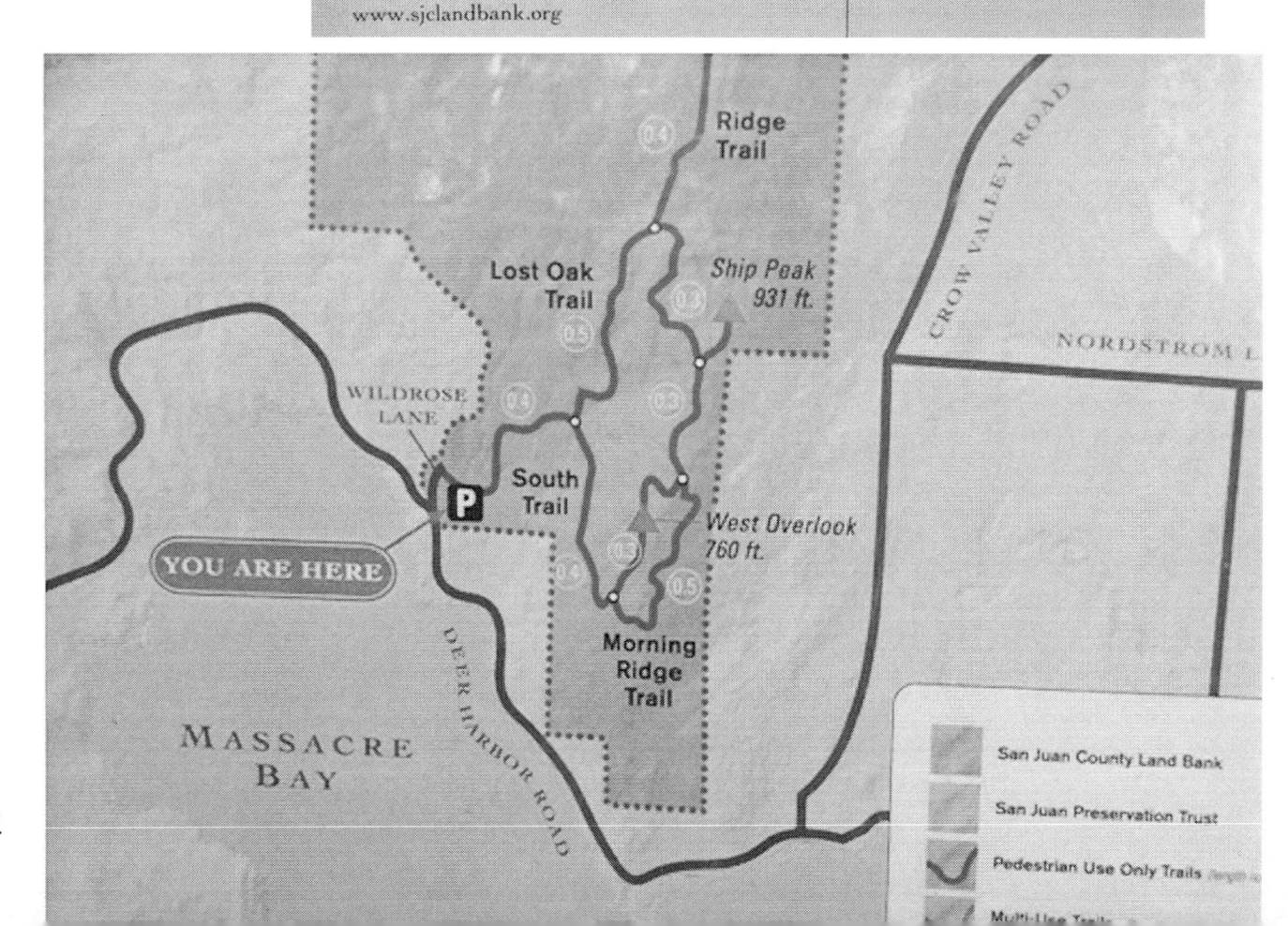

# Deer Harbor

$\mathcal{D}$eer Harbor Marina is at the end (almost) of Deer Harbor Rd. The marina boasts guest moorage for boats up to 120 feet, fuel, pump outs, potable water, electricity, wifi, and use of the pool. The dock store has groceries and a deli and grill.

The marina has boat, kayak, and bicycle rentals and can arrange for whale watching excursions. They offer a shuttle service to and from the Orcas ferry terminal. Lastly they offer laundry, shower and restrooms at the head of the gangway.

All you need to do is get yourself here, either by boat, by car, transit or their shuttle, the rest is easy. For slip assignment call Harbormaster on 78A or phone 360-376-3037

# Eastsound

Eastsound **the city** is one word, East Sound **the sound** is two words, Eastsound is located at the top end of East Sound. That settles the confusion I have. Eastsound is very definitely a city in spite of being promoted as a village. With houses and buildings dating to the 1800's, Eastsound really has pioneer roots. The downtown community is laid out in a modern-day grid with streets and sidewalks. Virtually all of the inner core area homes and building have been turned into shops, restaurants, galleries and bed and breakfast places. It's not all old – new and modern buildings fit nicely as do a few multi-story inns.

Just like Friday Harbor, the best way to explore and experience Eastsound is to park your vehicle and walk around. It is not very big, maybe three blocks by three blocks and parking is abundant.

Visit the Pioneer Museum at 181 North Beach Rd, rent kayaks, sign up for whale watch excursions, or if you are fortunate to be there on a Saturday, go to the Orcas Island Farmers Market on the Village Green in the middle of town. If you show up unexpected in the off season, you will easily find lodging, but I would go online and make a reservation to be sure.

The islands primary grocery store is located here, in fact, everything is here including the airport. Once we bought a new boat battery from the Napa store saving our vacation.

Live entertainment at the Village Green

The public restrooms are on Beach Rd in front of the Village Green.

**Main Street Eastsound really is called Main Street**

Virtually every old home has been converted to commercial use, there is civic pride bursting from every seam and facet of Eastsound. I think you will really enjoy your visit whether to grab some groceries and scurry back to the campground, or hang around the Saturday Farmers Market listening to island musicians beating out something that gets you going.

## Eastsound Dog Park

Get in the car, I know I just said to park your rig and walk around, but the airport and the dog park are half a mile north of downtown, even further if you come by boat, and that's a little further than I like to walk. The dog park is at the north end of town right by the airport. Follow Beach Rd (the same street the village green and museum are on) north until you get to Mt Baker Rd. The dog park is on the corner. Hopefully loud airplanes are someplace else when you stop by.

**This is a fenced - off leash park**

# Eastsound County Dock

$\mathcal{B}$oaters heading to Eastsound have reached the end of the road so to speak and are rewarded with a fairly nice dock, except you aren't allowed to overnight. All is not lost, you can anchor nearby and slumber away. Building waves blown all the way from Lopez Sound may very well interrupt you at 3am. Not to worry, you can anchor a short ways west (½ mi) in protected Judd Bay.

The smallish county dock may be overwhelmed by a single thirty foot cruiser on the outside and half a dozen dinghy's crowding the inside so I recommend that you plan on anchoring. If you get to claim a spot, that's great. When you anchor, be sure to respect the signs that say not to anchor in the eel grass beds north of the wharf.

It's a very short two block walk to the large *"Island Market"* grocery store. Simply walk down the road at the head of the gangway, cross Main St and the store is in the next block, very easy.

Tip Eastsound is a good place to rendezvous with bicycle riders or friends in cars. There is parking at the top of the gangway and cell phones work. One time we met up with riders that came from Anacortes on the 8:30 ferry, they made it to the dock by noon and we had plenty of time to ride around town before heading off to Jones Island for camping.

# West Beach Resort Marina

Just a little ways up the **north coast** on Orcas Island is West Beach Resort. They offer RV camping tent camping ,cabins, and slips for boats. If the slips are taken they have anchor buoys scattered offshore. The marina boasts a fuel dock and minimal grocery store where they bake their own waffle cones. West Beach Marina is very significant to boaters because they are the only place on the north side

of Orcas Island to buy fuel. They rent kayaks and powerboats, and have a boat launch if you brought yours on a trailer. I don't believe they monitor VHF so here is the phone number, 877 - 937 - 8224.

West Beach Resort is at 190 Waterfront way, Eastsound Wa 98245. Follow the roads from Orcas Landing towards Eastsound, just before Eastsound, keep left , do not turn down Main St, turn left on Enchanted Forest and follow to resort entrance signs.

By water , West Beach Marina is west of Point Doughty about 1 ½ miles and is protected on the east by its own small unnamed point.

TIP: All small water accessed places are extremely hard to spot from offshore, I strongly advise staying well out to sea and use field glasses to spot the marina before turning towards land.

# Rosario Resort

Rosario Resort has captured the hearts of romantics for years. Through good times and rough times it survives.  Beginning life as a ship builders palatial retirement home,  Rosario has  turned into a destination resort for boaters and non-boaters alike.

Some people believe that Rosario belongs at number three of the most important places to visit in the San Juans. Number two being Roche Harbor and number one Friday Harbor.

The mansion has been turned into a restaurant and popular wedding venue which I know little about, but all visitors need to know that the upstairs of the mansion houses a free museum with displays of early history when Robert Moran was building ships for the gold rush days. For this reason I urge everyone to stop by.

Originally Moran owned seven thousand acres on Orcas Island before donating thousands  to the state to become Moran State Park

He sold out in 1938, several owners later  in 1960 Rosario Resort and Spa opened.  The marina and breakwater came later, as did the less formal restaurant and store.

Rosario Mansion houses a museum upstairs as well as everything for a storybook wedding, including rental bungalows, private gardens and aristocratic yard games

Rosario marina and fuel docks

# For Boaters Going to Rosario

Rosario is located on Cascade Bay on the side of East Sound. Getting to the marina in your own boat is quite simple. Once in the inner island area, head up East Sound on Orcas Island (the inside of the horseshoe) favoring the north (right) side. At first on the right you will see Buck Bay and the community known as Olga, but you wont see any big mansions or a marina, keep going 2 ½ miles total. Rosario is the only choice. If you get to the end at Eastsound you will be three miles too far, turn around and try again.

Rosario Marina has a fuel pier which has room for boats off to one side not getting fuel. Room permitting they will let you stay for two hours complimentary. One time the attendant let us tie up for four hours while we rode our bicycles up to Moran State Park and Cascade Lake. It was a brutal uphill grind. We were back in four hours with smoking brakes.

I suggest you get fuel and then park the boat somewhere while you walk over to the mansion for a free tour of the museum upstairs. If you're hungry, drop into the Cascade Bay Grill overlooking the marina. Next to the restaurant is a fairly well stocked store, but be careful the prices might reflect the location.

If the fuel dock attendant can't hook you up with a slip, call the Harbormaster on 78A or try 360 376 2152. Our cell phones have never worked, and still didn't have any bars last visit back in 2014, so good luck.

## Cars and Bicyclists Headed to Rosario

Rosario Resort is at 1400 Rosario Rd, Eastsound, Wa 98245, the resorts number is 360-376-2222

To get to Rosario, get off the ferry at Orcas Landing and drive to Eastsound. Go though Eastsound following signs to Moran State Park. You will be on Olga Rd. About four miles beyond Eastsound but before entering the park you will see the Rosario sign and road to the right. It is easy to miss but the park will remind you to turn around.

San Juan Transit offers Rosario bus service to and from the ferry on weekends during the summer.

*- The San Juans consist of*
*750 islands at low tide*
*450 at high tide -*

# Moran State Park

Sixty years ago, our family camped at Cascade Lake in Moran State Park. I remember wanting to rent a sailing pram, but all I got was an inner tube. Not much has changed at the park but I finally got a sailing dinghy.

Today the park boasts five lakes, thirty eight miles of trails including one ½ half mile trail that leads to Rosario Resort. There are horse trails, mountain bike trails, trout fishing, kitchen shelters, some with electricity, 151 tent sites spread out in five different campgrounds, plus 15 primitive sites for hikers and bikers. Coin operated hot showers are in some of the restrooms.

There are two boat launches on Cascade Lake, but gas motors are not allowed. Some of the campsites can accommodate RV's up to 45 feet long.

The park concessionaires serve up snacks and rent rowboats, but you will need to bring your own bikes, kayaks and paddle boards.

A visit to Moran would not be complete without driving or hiking to the top of Mt Constitution. At 2409 feet it towers above the rest of the San Juans. Speaking of towers, on top is a stone tower you may walk up for an even better view. From the lofty top on a clear day one may see distant snow capped mountains in all directions. Vancouver Island is where the sun sets and somewhere between Mt Baker and Mt Rainier early birds may see it rise.

On a hot day - refreshing Cascade Lake is where the action is in 5200 acre Moran State Park.

The tower on top of Mt Constitution was under repair when we last visited, but it was a foggy evening anyway. We salvaged the ride up with a hair raising ride back down, 2400 feet to sea level in about five minutes is one way to vacation, I can think of others less exciting.

# Olga

Olga has seen more active times. The store has been closed for years and was for sale in 2016. Once upon a time they supported gas sales. Across the street is a dinky post office where they ask you not to leave your car idling while inside.

The gangway and wharf was a community effort. A few homes are full time but most are not. Up the hill a couple blocks, at the turn of the main road is a restaurant bakery that has a loyal following and is well reviewed. They exhibit works of local artists.

Out in Buck Bay past the dock are lots of private anchor buoys, but most will be empty, and in the middle of summer no less.

Fifty cents per foot is the best deal in the San Juans, but there aren't any takers today, nor are there restrooms or water. The good folks of Olga are to be commended for sharing their facility and welcoming travelers. Many places simply put out "No Trespassing" signs.

To find Olga follow Olga Rd from Eastsound through Moran Park, it ends at Olga.

🎯 **Tip** the fastest shortest way to bike up Mt Constitution, is to start at Olga if you come by boat. Rosario is a little bit closer, but you may only have two hours free parking at the dock.

# Obstruction Pass State Park

Obstruction Pass Park is a semi primitive walk in park. There is a quarter to half mile walk beyond the parking lot. To drive the point home, boaters will find that the campground is not on the water either, its hidden a short walk up a trail. The park includes shoreline of course, but the camping area is up in the woods.

To find the park follow Olga Rd south out of Eastsound, pass through Moran park and when you get to Olga turn left (The road curves around the restaurant) at Point Lawrence Rd after ½ mile, turn right on Obstruction Pass Rd, go another ¾ mile and turn right on to Trailhead Rd. It's a narrow gravel Road and has a sign saying Obstruction Pass Park. Check your miles, don't go too far or you will go way too far before you figure it out.

**For Boaters:** This park is hard to spot and the shore does not look inviting, but here are some landmarks to locate on your chart. The park is the unmarked point to the **left of Deer Point.** Plus, when you round the point, you will be able to see Olga and Buck Bay. If you can't see Olga you haven't rounded the point. Once you verify Olga, go back and anchor right behind the point. There is supposed to be an anchor buoy, but those things disappear. There is a leaning sign on the bank. Good luck.

This sign will not help you find the park because it is at the parking lot,

not out on the road where you are lost.

The park has nine tent sites and four bathrooms, and one site designated for kayakers. Remember its a walk in campground, so it is a great place for bicycle campers packing all their gear.

This is also a great place to drop by and picnic while hiking around the forty wooded acres and public shoreline. From out on the point you have views of Olga and Rosario in the distance.

The leaning sign you will see **from the boat**, it's your only clue to finding the park

### 🎯 Hazard warning

This is a potentially stormy lee shore. I would not anchor here overnight. See all the driftwood in the picture? Even if you don't have nasty weather or drag onto the beach while you slumber, you will have big wakes from skippers blasting through Peavine and Obstruction Pass. I suggest moving around the point to Olga or Rosario.

*Doe Island before storm destroyed float*

## Doe Island State Park

*I* hesitated including Doe Island because the state has chose to shut it down and does not appear to be in any hurry to open it up.

Before it was closed, it only amounted to an acre or two with one campsite and one horrible pit privy.

Triggering the closure was a storm that damaged the float. As of 2016 it was still missing in action.

Doe Island is very close to Orcas Island, only a stones throw away and about two miles north of Obstruction Pass.

It's still a good place to anchor in the lee, and you can always dinghy to shore for a ten minute walk-about.

## Did you know that the San Juan Islands are much older than the mainland, and are really sunken mountain tops?

### Clark Island State Park

Clark Island is a drive-by island park, meaning boaters hurry by on their way somewhere else, such as Sucia or Matia. It's not much more than a narrow speed bump in Rosario Strait between Lummi and Orcas Island. There are fifteen campsites and a composting toilet. On the Rosario Strait side is a small group of anchor buoys that are protected from south swell, but not from the north. The west side of Clark has one buoy and is subject to swift currents. Being in the middle of Rosario Strait leaves the island subject to winds other parks may not notice. In 2016 we looked for hiking trails on Clark and could not find any going to north end.

**Hazard warning:** the anchor buoy field on the east side is partially surrounded by a charted under water hook shaped reef that skippers must locate and avoid.

**Kayak Tip:** Taking advantage of the Rosario Strait tidal current makes Clark an easy overnight destination choice for paddlers putting in at Washington Park in Anacortes.

### Matia Island State Park

Matia Island rivals Jones Island for my number one choice. Matia is located off the north coast of Orcas almost in a line between Clark and Sucia. Only 1 ½ miles from Sucia and 3 ½ miles from Clark, Matia is in a world of its own. Rolfe inlet on its NW end has a four boat float and two anchor buoys. Surprisingly, we seem to always find room at the dock. About 2010 fire pits and open fires were banned curbing our enthusiasm for overnighters. Matia is unique from the other islands in that it has a rainforest type feeling with a one mile hike that immerses one in a shaded world of giant plants, ferns, mosses and massive trees. An hour long hike is truly awe inspiring, affecting the very soul. Matia is a good place to come back to .

Matia Island float

# Sucia Island State Park
## Quick Check
### *Echo Bay - Fossil Bay - Shallow Bay - Fox Cove - Ewing Cove - Snoring Cove*

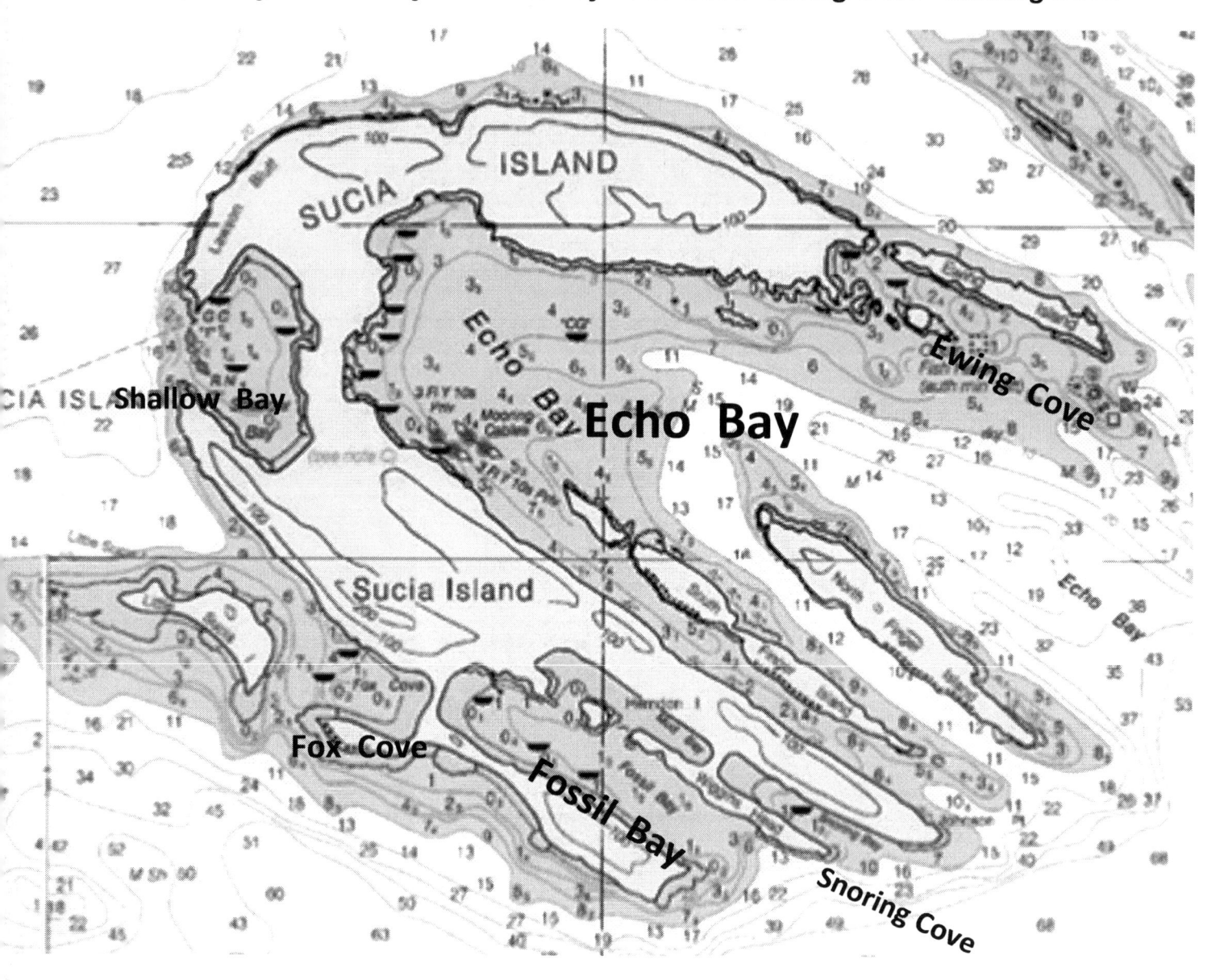

You don't just go to Sucia Marine Park, you go to a place at Sucia.

Similar to Stuart Island but with many more watery fingers to explore, Sucia was a smugglers haven back when smuggling was a way of life.

I'm going to rattle off important trivia I think you will appreciate knowing.

The main campground is on the narrow isthmus between Fox Cove and Fossil Bay. Hiking trails connect all the bays and coves from end to end. It is fairly easy to get disoriented (lost) and tired, bring some water and a lunch when you explore. Fossil Bay is the only place with docks and running water. All the coves listed have bathrooms and pay stations. All the bays have protected nice anchoring except Fox which has strong tidal current, and Shallow Bay which has rolling wake swells from ships in Boundary Pass. Fox Cove, Shallow Bay and Fossil Bay have poor dinghy beaches. Note: A poor dinghy beach is not steep enough to get you to shore without your wishing you hadn't attempted keeping your hiking shoes dry. Tip - wear sandals.

98

Left half of Echo Bay - if you squint you can see ever-present Mt. Baker in this hazy late afternoon picture.

One of two Fossil Bay floats

Sucia has a long history of drug running, rum smuggling, and transporting illegal immigrants. Since becoming a state park things have cooled off but who knows what's going on in the boat next door.

Echo Bay is huge with lots and lots of easy anchoring . It's also very popular as a rendezvous place for party animals and boating clubs.

Sucia is tremendously popular as a destination for kayakers and kayak camping. Many outfitters lead tours to Sucia. There is a concessionaire at Fossil Bay that rents kayaks.

There are group camp sites and single sites you may reserve by calling the local rangers, that live at the park. Call 360 376 2073 or go to their web site at http://parks.state.wa.us/594/Sucia-Island

All the bays and coves have anchoring systems and buoys. Snoring, Fox,and Ewing only have room for a few boats which means you will be blessed with tranquility and quiet - maybe.

Echo Bay

Ewing Cove

Lineal tie ups at Echo Bay are a little high for dinghies

Lineal tie ups at Echo Bay are higher than many boats

Echo Bay is great for Dinghy Sailing

## Patos Island Marine Park

𝒫atos is as far north as you can go before entering Canada, and this desolate looking lighthouse attests to that, but on a less gloomy note, the rest of the island park is very nice.

Lighthouses are adopted by volunteers and like Stuart's Turn Point Lighthouse, Patos has it own admiring group. They line up all summer for the chance to spend a week camping in the woods so they may host visiting tourists. Inside the building are the usual old photos and news clipping about past keepers and their exploits. The stairway to the top is open and you may climb up and look at the automated light.

From the campground at the head of the anchorage it only takes ten minutes to walk out on a mostly concrete path left over from the Coast Guard days. If you prefer you may run your dinghy about halfway out and put in at a small beach where an old concrete side trail was used to access supply boats.

There are seven very private woodsy campsites with tables and fire rings, the usual composting privy sums it up. The beach area has tables and ring for day use.

There is a somewhat boring 1.5 mile loop through the woods leaving most of the island and park natural and without trails.

The anchoring bay is not a true bay and has a tidal current that needs to be respected during stormy conditions. The parks department reports many boats have dragged anchor with a north wind and swell.

**Poor judgment warning:** Most boaters arrive from Sucia and points south so they are presented with the option of running the gap between Patos and Little Patos Islands to save ten minutes versus continuing around Little Patos and entering from the north. Even though I go through the little channel sometimes myself, I recommend that you do not unless you are an experienced gunk-holer, and then only dead slow with the current in your face. The side clearance is just a few feet and the depth changes with the tide.

The bay at Patos has only two anchor buoys so most of the boats are swinging on the hook.

We use Patos as our jump off point when going to Vancouver or north. When returning and checking in at customs late in the day at Point Roberts (12 miles north), it is nice to come home to a place we are familiar with.

## Inati Bay

While not part of the defined San Juans or even a public park, all skippers need to know about Inati Bay on Lummi Island. Why? Because it is a safe harbor and sometimes we need one.

Inati Bay is on the southern eastern side of Lummi Island, it's almost exactly two miles north of the southern tip of the island on the Bellingham side. The hooked entrance bay is clear of any rocks and has deep water close to shore making anchoring easy. The shore is a gravely beach once leased to the Bellingham Yacht club, I have heard differing stories whether visitors are currently welcome on shore. In any case, it is a great lunch stop on a sunny day or a place to reduce sails or just wait out a blow on Bellingham Bay. Boaters traveling to the San Juans from Squalicum Harbor transit quite near Inati Bay and may not know of its existence. I suggest marking it on your chart, or even taking a quick look when you have extra time.

**Hazard warning:** There is a marked and charted rock just outside the bay, be sure to locate it and go around either side.

# Cypress Island

Sometimes what makes a great destination is one amenity or one fantastic experience. I think repeatable good times cement a places reputation, Cypress delivers.

Cypress Island is really big and most of it is undeveloped Department of Natural Resources land (DNR) It is not technically part of the San Juans, nor is it a State Park. There is private land scattered around with some homes on the west shore facing Rosario Strait in a cove called Strawberry Bay. Kayakers and small boat boaters heading out from Anacortes are able to reach Cypress without crossing Rosario Strait making it a very attractive lunch or overnight destination. Cruising type boaters pass by (go around) Cypress on their way to and from the San Juans, the lucky ones make it part of their travels.

For our tourist purposes there are three places on Cypress to consider, all are on the east side facing Bellingham Channel.

### Pelican Beach - Eagle Harbor - Cypress Head

Pelican Beach is at the north end of Cypress. It is a DNR campground so there are no fees, that's right its free, don't ask why, I don't know. There are seven camp sites and six anchor buoys. All the sites are right on the beach with fire rings etc. It is not unusual for us to count two dozen kayaks and all the buoys taken when we arrive late in the day. We have found we can easily squeeze in and anchor close to shore, avoiding the current further out.

The prior page is an image of the Pelican Beach community shelter and fire ring, plus ADA approved wheelchair ramps leading to the composting toilets. Note: there is no dock, but the beach is very dinghy friendly.

Hiking trails begin at the shelter leading to Eagle Bluff lookout, Smugglers Cove, Duck Lake, and connect with other trails leading to the reclaimed airstrip, Cypress Lake etc.

Note: the trail to Eagle Bluff is closed each year until after July 15 so hikers do not disturb nesting eagles.

🎯 Tip: The Eagle Bluff hike is our favorite in the San Juans, (possibly equal to Matia) we don't miss a chance to come back. It takes about two hours to drop anchor, dinghy to shore, hike up and back, dinghy back, up anchor and continue on our way. I highly recommend it, the view is worth the effort.

*E*agle Harbor is a fairly well protected anchorage with around twenty buoys. It is one mile south of Pelican Beach. If you are unable to secure a spot at Pelican Beach, this is where you go in a pinch.

The bad news, is that Eagle Harbor does not have much to offer other than a handy place to get a buoy or anchor. The swampy shallow beach is not easy to land dinghy's and the little pit toilet is hard to find back in the woods. One redeeming value though is that once you do get to shore, you have access to the trail system. Eagle Harbor is your best (shortest) access point for hiking to Cypress Lake, which is about two miles one way and uphill.

*C*ypress Head is a little teensy island connected to Cypress with a narrow isthmus barely above storm waters. It is one and a half miles south of Eagle Harbor. Cypress head campground has five sites with fire rings and a composting toilet, but being out on a point (island) subjects the sites to wind otherwise not noticed. Crossing the short isthmus allows access to the trails on Cypress. The shortest hike to the abandoned airstrip is from Cypress Head.

Cypress Head and the isthmus effectively creates two coves for anchoring, the northern one has two buoys and a nice gravely dinghy beach. The southern cove will be calm when the north cove is frothy, offering a handy alternative.

Kayakers from Anacortes easily ride the currents back and forth in Bellingham Channel making Cypress a very popular destination. Kayakers need to give the Head extra clearance during heavy flood and ebb due to nasty eddies and standing waves.

This Cypress Head campsite might be a little breezy, but what an awesome view in all directions

## Why Cypress Island?

For some, Cypress Island is a destination. For others it's just a stop on the way to somewhere else.

Some come for recreation— to hike, camp, fish, hunt or view wildlife.

Some seek solitude and peace— a haven from fast-paced lives elsewhere—hoping to find inspiration and spiritual renewal.

Why are YOU here?

WE ARE THE CHILDREN OF OUR LANDSCAPE; IT DICTATES BEHAVIOR AND EVEN THOUGHT IN THE MEASURE TO WHICH WE ARE RESPONSIVE TO IT.
—LAWRENCE DURRELL

# Saddlebag Island State Marine Park

Saddlebag is small at only 24 acres, but it is the familiar dogbone shape (or saddlebag shape) giving it lots of shoreline and two coves. On shore are five campsites on the narrow isthmus. You can make the figure eight hike in about thirty minutes and the trail is fairly easy, although it is becoming somewhat overgrown, probably due to lack of use. The north cove is where to anchor. Inside the cove is room for only two or three boats if they stern tie to reduce swing, There is plenty of anchor room outside the cove and you needn't worry about passing wakes because there are few passing boats.

Saddlebag is located on the east side of Guemes Island, just two miles past Anacortes and Cap Sante. From the hiking trails is an unobstructed south view of the Anacortes refinery, fortunately from the anchorage you are looking north.

Saddlebag is conveniently located for a lunch stop when running through Swinomish Channel or when we find ourselves losing daylight and no chance of making our original planned overnight spot. Several times it has been our "go to island" causing me to comment, *"you can count on Saddlebag."*

The cove holds one or two boats, the beach is fairly steep making dry feet a sure thing when landing the dinghy. We enjoy campfires at the beachfront fire rings talking into the dark.

*"You can count on Saddlebag"*

Using currents to advantage is common sense, and when paddling a kayak may make or break an outing. Saddlebag Island is an easy destination or waypoint when putting in at Washington Park or Cap Sante.

# Swinomish Channel

*T*he Channel is a godsend for some boaters avoiding Deception Pass. Deception Pass isn't necessarily a bad thing to avoid, all boats easily go through at slack water, its the fog and big waves lurking out in the Strait of Juan de Fuca and Rosario Strait that are to be avoided. They're the bad thing, and even then only on bad days. Swinomish channel is mostly man made with an interesting history, but I won't rob anyone of discovering their own local area knowledge artifacts. For our purposes you need to know that the channel is maintained to a depth of twelve feet and is several hundred feet wide for its entire eleven mile length. Another consideration is the current. Twin engine power cruisers with big fuel tanks blast both ways oblivious to the current, but puttsterss and sailboats are forewarned to plan to go with the flow which may be up to three miles per hour in places. The entire channel is a no wake zone, but seems to get ignored by lots of skippers. Predicting the flow direction and velocity seems to be a crap shoot defying wisdom, I wish I knew what to suggest. The local joke is that the channel flows one way for 23 hrs and then reverses, and nobody knows when. My experience is that it always flows the opposite way I'm going and the slower my boat the faster the current. I try to stay at the seawall in La Conner until I see it going my way.

Hazard warning: Both ends of Swinomish Channel are dredged out of mud bays for the last few miles. You must not leave the marked channel until you clear the final nav. aids. There is a real desire to cut the corner so to speak, especially when a local fisherman does it in front of you and gets away with it.

There is no room to go on the wrong side of any markers. To make a believer of you, go through at low tide, then you will see what those small numbers on your chart stand for.

# La Conner

*I*f you don't make La Conner a part of your travels, you are missing the boat, or RV as the case may be. The main street you want to visit is only two or three blocks, you walk down one side and up the other. Why not?

Local artistic shops and galleries line both sides sharing wall to wall early day buildings with eateries. Behind the waterfront buildings is a brand new public esplanade, at places suspended over the water. The esplanade runs the full length of downtown and provides access to three public floats for overnighter transient boaters. Pay at the kiosk at the head of the gangway. On main street is a public restroom only a few yards from the docks.

We make it a point to search out museums when we visit places, especially old places. La Conner is the home of two that I like. The Skagit County Historical Museum is at 501 S 4th which places it up on the hill above main street. You can drive your car around the somewhat steep roads, or if you are on foot because your boat is tied to the dock, look for a stairway to the left of the rest rooms.

Some people are fond of quilts and weaving so the La Conner Quilt and Textile Museum at 703 2nd is a must see one block walk. I admit I find it interesting.

Further down the channel a quarter mile in a northward direction is the La Conner Marina and fuel dock. They have month to month slips and 2400 feet of transient space, and two pump out docks.

The marina has a fork lift sling for under 7500 lb boats and a full size travel lift available. You are well advised to call for information and reservations for any services - 613 North 2nd St La Conner Wa 98257

Call harbormaster on channel 66A or try 360 466 3118 - I don't think you will go wrong with La Conner

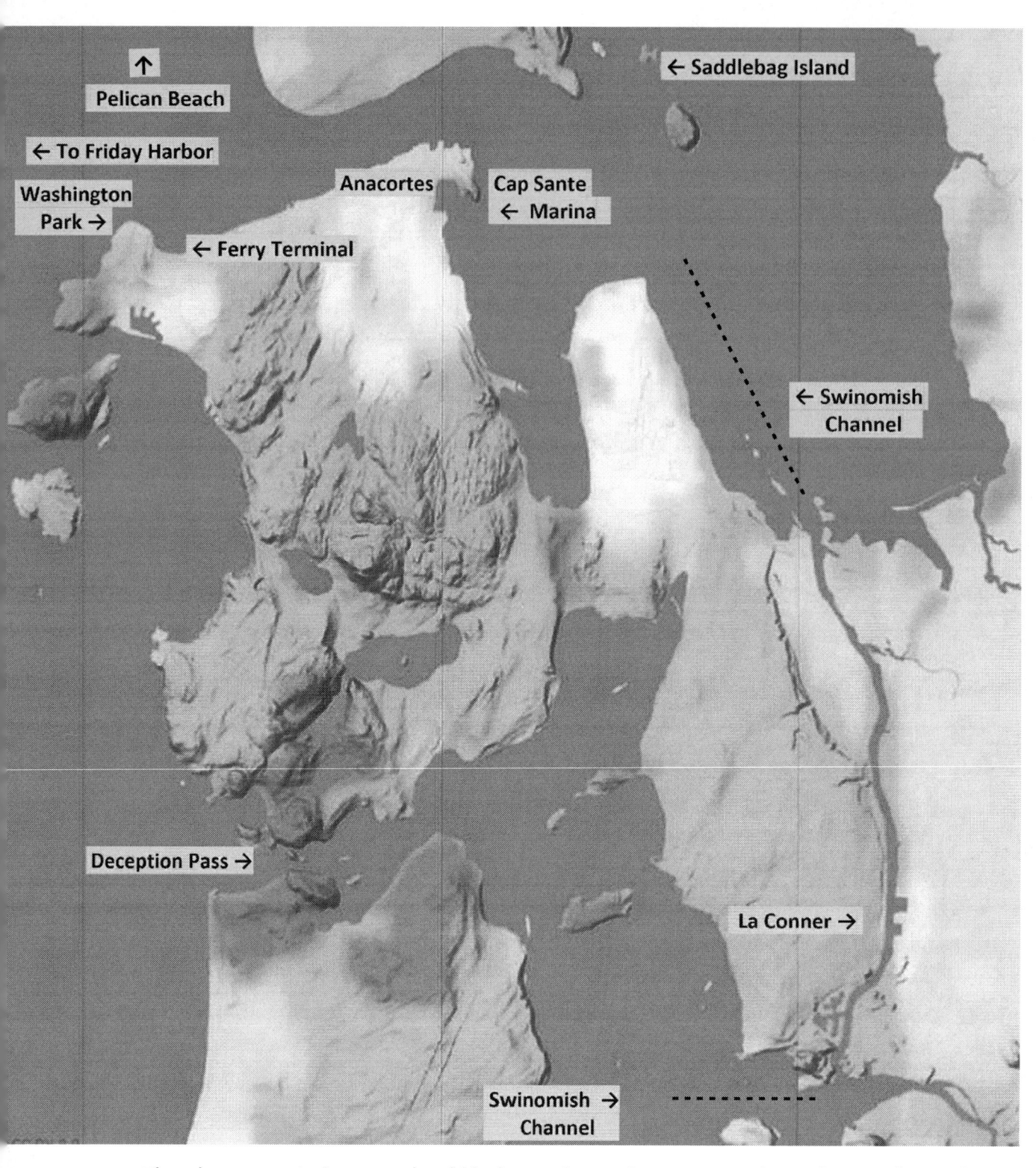

The above proximity map should help you locate important points when making plans.

Swinomish Channel = 11 miles long
La Conner to Deception Pass = 9 mi
La Conner to Cap Sante Marina = 9.5 mi
Anacortes to Deception Pass = 6 hwy mi
Washington Park to Saddlebag Park = 5.5 mi

Washington Park to Pelican Beach = 6.5 mi
Washington Park to James Island = 3.5 mi
Cap Sante Marina to Saddlebag Island = 2.5 mi
Cap Sante to Friday Harbor = 19.5
Cap Sante to Sucia = 21 mi

Eleven mile long Swinomish Channel includes two to three miles of dredged mud flats at each end.

# Deception Pass State Park (marine park)

### Cornet Bay - Bowman Bay - Sharpe Cove - Rosario Beach

*I* urge everyone to visit Deception Pass by car if you can. I have no comments on the campgrounds (except there are several). While you are driving in on the main road you should stop and park your vehicle up on the cliffs just north of the bridge, or the very best place to park is the small parking area on Pass Island. That's the spot in between the two bridges.

From this central parking spot you can walk out on both sides and spend a while just watching. Pretty soon boats will come through to amaze you with how the swirling currents affect them. There is a trail under the bridge on Pass Island allowing you to get a little closer, but don't fall in. This is a very treacherous place to get rescued from the water on a good day, on a bad day – well just be careful.

On the south shore immediately off the bridge is a parking lot and bathrooms. There is a trailhead leading down to the beach far below, but I want you to hike up to Goose Rock Summit viewpoint at the top. Its only four tenths of a mile and is an easy romp. The views on a clear day are of the San Juans, Victoria and the Olympic mountains. You can also access this trail by taking a dinghy ride across Cornet bay and bushwhacking straight up hill until you cross the perimeter trail in about thirty feet. Watch the tide and make sure the dinghy is tied well. When doing the bushwhack dinghy trip, do not paddle past Ben Ure Island or risk getting involved with Deception Pass cliffs and currents.

Under the bridge on Pass Island are trails and vistas worth the two minute hike. Bring lunch, find a place to sit, you will enjoy your stop.

## Cornet Bay

Cornet Bay is part of Deception Pass Park, and is for boaters, oh you can park your RV or car in the parking lot and fish from the docks but the parks department built the ramps, floats, and wharves for boaters to launch and overnight. It's a great facility where we have enjoyed many days and nights. Cornet Bay is just around the corner from the pass barely a half mile away. Passing boats send their wakes into the bay so it is not perfect, but it is close.

Adjacent to the overnight floats is a four lane all tide launching ramp. At the top of the ramp is an oversized trailer parking lot and an overflow lot. You will never see them filled, never. The water fountain has been turned off as long as I can remember, even since the big remodel, but the sink in the restroom works and you can slip a small saucepan under it. There is no water on the dock. The Cornet Bay Store is about a thousand foot walk.

This is a fine jump off place to the San Juans, or to hang out a few days, or just a few hours waiting for slack water or the fog to lift in the pass. With Swinomish Channel only five miles south, Cornet Bay gives you the option of ducking through the channel should the weather close in. It's a good place.

## Bowman Bay

Bowman has lots to offer visitors. Like Cornet Bay it's in Deception Pass Park, but lets make sure we understand where things are.

The pass is under the double bridge, Cornet Bay is a half mile **inside** and behind a small island, Bowman Bay is a half mile on the **outside**, on the other side behind a little point. The pass is narrowest directly under the bridge and that is why the current speeds up sometimes 9-10 mph for a short 500 foot distance. If you are inbound in a 6 mph sailboat, you can pull into Bowman Bay and wait an hour or four. So while you are waiting, why not dinghy ashore or tie up at the Sharpe Cove dock. I use Bowman Bay and Sharpe Cove names interchangeably, they are the left and right ends of the same place. Once on shore you can hike up to the bridge or skirt along the edge of calm and picturesque Lottie Bay on your way out to Lighthouse Point. (There is no lighthouse at Lighthouse Point.) If hiking is boring, try the interpretive center next to the campground.

## Sharpe Cove

Getting to the dock is straight forward, just don't run into the awash well charted rocks that form an annoying partial barrier between the two bays. The dock holds about four cruisers but don't be surprised to find some runabouts beat you there. On shore are trails to Bowman and the bridge. It's ok to spend the night, there is a pay station on the dock. There are four anchor buoys in Bowman Bay and the water will be smoother, but you will be directly in front of the campground. If being on public display bothers you, you can anchor on the far side.

## Rosario Beach

When you are driving out the main highway looking for Deception Pass, the first sign you come to will not say Deception Pass but Rosario Road and Rosario Beach. Turn – it takes you down to the Bowman Bay Campground road as well as Rosario Beach, but it is part of Deception Pass Park. Rosario Beach is across the little isthmus from Sharpe Cove taking about sixty seconds to walk from your boat or car. The beach, tide pools and waters are an acclaimed marine preserve and is home to the Rosario Beach Marine Laboratory.

Did I mention the sunsets from the Sharpe Cove point? It's another sixty second walk out to the bluff. The only better perch for watching orange and yellow sky's might be Deception Pass Bridge or Goose Rock Summit above the bridge, but its hard to beat a one minute walk.

Sharpe Cove float above - if you squint you can see the Maiden of Deception Pass at the top of the gangway

Maiden of Deception Pass

## Four lane Cornet Bay Ramps

Once you get launched, take a spot at the transient boaters dock. You have to pay for launching, parking and staying at the dock so it seems like the state is hitting you three times. They are, but its home. The ramp is first rate having four lanes and three finger floats, plus it is good for all tide levels.

The picture shows only half the main dock. Beyond the dock are more floats that require dinghy access to and from the main dock and shore.

Fishing is always a popular pastime on the docks at Cornet Bay

When you pull out of Cornet Bay heading through the pass, this is your view. Deception Pass is on the left and narrow S shaped Canoe Pass is on the right.

🎯 **Hazard warning:** Canoe Pass is navigable but you must attempt it <u>only with the current in your face and with a powerful responsive boat.</u> If you attempt to run with the current you will most certainly slam your vessel into the cliff at the S Curve.

In this image, Bowman Bay is past the bridge on the right side, the San Juans are straight ahead. The main passage is plenty wide for boats to pass each other. The pass is a straight shot and spooky deep. Depending on the speed of the tidal flow, you will encounter standing waves and swirly whirlpools tugging your keel for a short distance under the bridge. If you are <u>riding with a fast current</u> (same direction) in an under powered boat you will have to ride it out, there will be no turning back. You may bury your nose in a few standing waves. An open bow skiff is a big mistake, but a decked sailboat can easily take waves on the nose so stay off the deck and have a camera ready. If you try to go through and the current is too strong your boat will simply cease making headway. If you are directly under the bridge when you stall out, you might still make it by reading the swirlys and lifting your dinghy, fenders, and feet out of the water. If you can get just fifty feet either side of the bridge, the current slacks a little and you are home free, otherwise go back to Cornet Bay or Bowman Bay and wait it out.

Don't forget to look up and wave to the tourists cheering for you from the bridge.

*I don't want anyone to get the idea that this is a place where you can let down your guard and just have at it, on the contrary, Deception Pass demands your total attention and utmost respect. For many skippers, the best advice is to wait for slack water.*

***I don't like to endorse private enterprise but let's make an exception.*** This excursion boat is stationed at the Cornet Bay docks right next to where all of us tie up. They take loads of tourists out for one hour rides through the pass including Canoe Pass when the conditions are suitable. They get up close, providing great photo ops as well as informing guests about local history and some lore of the area.

During my stays at the Cornet Bay docks I have spoken with tour guests and the *Island Whaler* crew, everyone has reported wonderful and exciting outings. I have watched and listened to tourists pile off the boat walking past my boat all animated and excited. To me, that's the best of all possible reviews.

They sell tickets up on the bridge at the booth in the south end parking lot or you can get reservations at this number. Deception Pass Tours - 888-909-8687

I'm just reporting what I have seen and heard.

# Hope Island - Skagit Island - Goat Island - Fort Whitman

While we are in the Deception Pass area we should not leave out some lesser known sites.

These three islands are south of Deception Pass with Goat Island being the furthest at five miles.

Cornet Bay and Bowman Bay are popular kayak launching places, so it is no surprise that the three islands are popular destinations.

**Skagit Island is a** state marine park and is two miles from the Cornet dock and at about 24 acres is smallish, but it's not a dog bone shape so it has no coves, in fact the only beach you can safely land a kayak or dinghy is barely thirty feet wide. Most of the island shoreline is made up of cliffs or rocky shore. On the far east end is a single camp site adjacent the gravel beach. Standard pit toilet, picnic table, fire ring, and fee pay post is all there is.

Kayakers may find the place adorable but I had a hard time fighting the current in my dinghy and I was tenuously anchored at best. The twenty minute hiking trail follows the shore but at several places the cliff has fallen away leaving a nasty fall potential.

The only landable beach on Skagit Island is opposite the single camp site

**I want to warn everyone to watch young kids, there are places where the overgrown salal effectively hides drop offs into the ocean and deep water.**

**Hope Island** is also a state marine park half mile further and is much bigger at over a hundred acres. There is a little hook of a point creating a cove with several anchor buoys, but its distance from the main flow of north south traffic is what makes it a quiet and nice place. There is no noticeable current in the cove making anchoring and kayak paddling enjoyable too. On shore are three gravel beach front sites with fire rings and all that campers expect, plus some nice big overhanging trees for great rope swings.

There is supposed to be a cross island hiking trail, but I looked for it and could not find any indication where it begins. I'm guessing that since the island is mostly off limits due to being a sensitive ecosystem preserve that the rangers have let the trail return to nature and that's that.

We see boats anchored overnight here quite a bit. They are close enough to Cornet Bay to make ice runs but far enough away to really be alone.

**Goat Island and Fort Whitman** are five miles from Cornet Bay and part way up the Swinomish Channel dredged entrance making 90 acre Goat Island only three miles from La Conner.  That also makes La Conner a  spot to launch kayaks.  The city ramp and parking lot under the Rainbow bridge is a perfect place to begin a kayak expedition, but there are no official camp sites on Goat Island, so plan to continue on or return the same day.  (Unofficially there is evidence of beach camping on the south east side)

Goat Island is part of the Skagit Wildlife Area and is managed by the Washington Dept. Of Fish and wildlife.  Visiting is allowed but they don't promote it, or talk about it.

The island is public and has been a local attraction for generations of kids so many trails are scattered around.  Southern facing beaches  are sandy and driftwood covered waiting for someone to make a shelter, but Fort Whitman is the real attraction.  The fort is a concrete gun emplacement (Battery) dating to before world war one.  The plan was to protect the lower Puget Sound by firing 100 pound shells at war ships dumb enough to try coming through Deception Pass.  Like all the big gun batteries from back then, Fort Whitman was only used for practice.

Battery Emplacements at Fort Whitman

Finding Goat Island is easy, it's out in the mud flats alongside the Swinomish Channel, about three miles from La Conner.  But finding Fort Whitman requires directions.  Here goes – begin by heading up the channel like you are going from Cornet Bay to La Conner.  One mile up on your right is Goat Island just like your chart reads.  Also, on your right are lots of pilings and possibly stored log rafts.  What you want to do is look at the rows and rows of pilings **spotting the <u>only group</u> that has lots of rusty metal brackets at the top.** Those brackets were part of an old wharf. Now anchor your boat or tie to a piling and dinghy to shore **directly behind the pilings with brackets.** At high tide the beach is almost nonexistent but put in there anyway, and tie your painter to an overhanging tree. Next, bushwhack straight up the bank erring a little to the right and you will come to a trail or old road. Turn right and in a few hundred feet you will emerge at the edge of the battery.

Try to imagine the Fort without all the trees, neatly dug into the hill to be invisible sitting atop the cliff.

With some more bushwhacking you can look for evidence of more structures scattered around. For instance a thousand feet to the west near the tip of Goat Island is a fire range lookout building, instrumental in accurately aiming the guns. Have fun and bring a flashlight. Oh yeah – don't forget about your boat and dinghy down below with the changing current and tide, they may shift around some.

## Anacortes

Chances are you will be in Anacortes at the beginning or end of your visit if you are a car traveler. I suggest that you plan some time to explore, even a few hours will be worth it. What I like to do is catch the ferry in the morning, but I arrive as early as I can the day before. I rest up and look around town the afternoon I arrive.

Widely billed as the *Gateway to the San Juans*, except Anacortes isn't even in the same county. I do agree with the billing, but only because the ferry terminal is located there and Guemes channel is a straight shot to *Thatcher Pass*. (Possibly the real gateway)

I recommend visitors set aside some time for exploring Anacortes and the area.

**Here's some Anacortes local knowledge, please use it or lose it.**

- Drive or hike from the marina to the top of Cap Sante Park, the sunrise and sunset views are spectacular. Cap Sante is the big rocky outcrop rising 300 feet above town. It's only a one mile walk or drive. You will have a 360 degree view of the San Juans, Mt Baker and miles of bays, straits and water channels.
- Tour the historical sternwheeler snagboat – WT Preston. It's on the hard across from the Cap Sante Marina parking lot.
- Go to Rosario Beach and Deception Pass, walk out on the bridge. It would be a shame to miss Deception Pass when it is only six miles from the ferry terminal.

After missing morning coffee Linda considers jumping off Cap Sante

### WT Preston  *Snag-boat*

- For the canine crew, visit Ace of Hearts Rotary Dog Park (off leash and fenced) 38th & H Ave. in Anacortes.
- Run over to La Conner, it's only ten miles and you can cut through the Swinomish reservation on reservation road using the Rainbow bridge. How cool is that?
- There is much more in Anacortes, but these places deserve your scrutiny.

## Cap Sante Marina

Cap Sante Marina is where most boaters think to go when looking for a place to launch their boat in Anacortes. I've already given directions for the ferry terminal, Cap Sante will be the same route except when you get into the center of town at the Safeway you will turn right. That's it.

For your GPS try this >> 1019 Q Ave. Anacortes, Wa 98221   (360) 293-0694 - VHF - 66a

They don't have a ramp, they have two slings, a big full size travel lift that requires reservations in advance. They also have a smaller first come first served small boat rig. This is a busy but efficient place. Once your boat is dunked in the water you will be expected to move it away immediately, not begin to load it with supplies. You should make arrangements for temporary space before hand.

At the far end of the parking lot is a long term lot for your trailer and vehicle. They also have a section for RV's where you can spend the night. Across the street is Safeway and down the street one block is West Marine.

For Ramp launching, go to Washington Park, Cornet Bay, La Conner, or Squalicum Harbor. Twin Bridges is not a preferred ramp in my opinion. There are no other ramps that I know of except Oak Harbor, and that's a little too far away.

Cap Sante seems go on forever and there is always something going on.
Out at the breakwater is a floating pump out station.
Outside the picture to the left is a long term boat trailer and RV parking lot
Across the street is Safeway.  (Starbucks inside on our last visit.)

# Washington Park

Washington Park is an Anacortes City Park, but don't let it's ownership influence you. The city also owns Cap Sante and both places are first rate.

To get there follow the signs to the ferry terminal and keep going another mile to the end of the road. The park has 68 campsites nestled in its 220 acres of forest making it quite a bit larger than some of the islands we visit in the San Juans.

At the beginning of the park is a concrete two lane all tides ramp. They have limited parking with a little overflow field up by the park entrance. Before you launch they suggest that you make sure where you will park. Note: in a pinch you could run your car and trailer down to the ferry terminal where they have several long term parking lots.

Many of the campground sites have oversize driveways suitable for trailer parking after launching. You may camp, or launch your boat and park your car and trailer for up to 14 days.

🎯 Tip: If you have a ski boat that is not suitable for camping aboard, consider making Washington Park your home base in the San Juans. Take off for the islands each day and return each night, or take off for a couple days, you decide. Fourteen days is a long time living out of a cooler and a sleeping bag, but there are worse things than not dealing with ferry traffic. I would take my runabout to the San Juans in a heartbeat.

If you want to kayak or go kayak camping, make Washington Park your launch site. Cypress Island, Saddlebag Island, James Island, are easy paddles, but all of the San Juans are within your reach.

Reservation web site for Washington Park
http://anacortesparksandrecreation.sportsites.com/Reservation/ReservationStep1.aspx?id=2326

Washington Park two lane ramp and float

# James Island Marine Park

Another dogbone island, that's a good thing, it means two coves to choose from.

All of James is a state park, it's only 113 acres. The hiking trails are only on the south side summit and along the shore. There are several thirty minute loop hikes. The summit trail has a great view overlooking the cove and out towards Thatcher Pass. The shoreline hike along the southern shore is a little tricky with some nasty drop off spots.

🎯 I don't recommend the south shore trail for the **infirmed, inebriated or clumsy.**

There are three campgrounds with 13 camp sites total, three sites are just for kayakers and motor less sailing crafts. All the campgrounds have the usual park service composters and fire rings.

The east cove faces Rosario Strait so it is subject to wakes from boats to and from Thatcher Pass. We stop by often and I notice they have added more anchor buoys. There may be four or five now.

The west cove has a four boat dock and no anchor buoys, but setting the hook is easy enough and there is room for three or four boats. I have seen retractable keel sailboats on the gravel beach.

If Rosario fog gives you pause, make your way into James to wait it out. James is the first place to relax for kayakers shooting across the four miles from Washington Park. Many times James is the last place we visit before surrendering and going home. We tend to hang out as long as we can, delaying our departure as long as possible. In my inner thoughts I am looking for or hoping for a reason to stay.

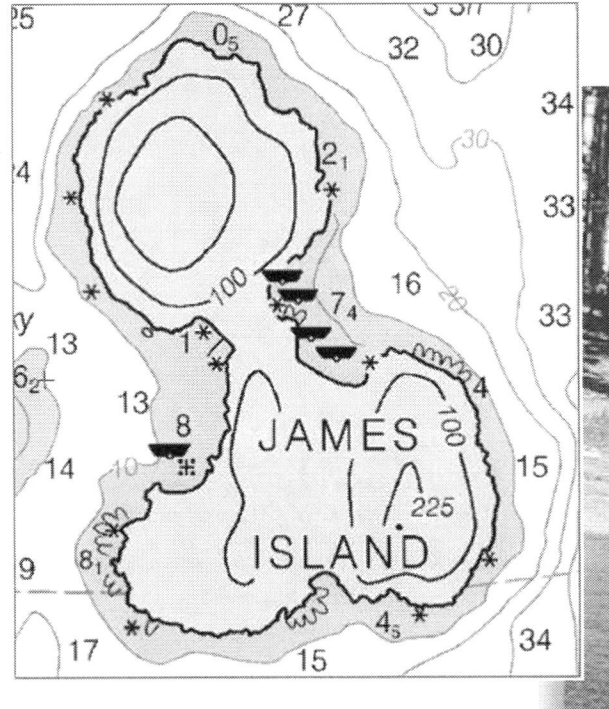

# Blakely's

On the far north end of Blakely Island on the inside of Peavine Pass, is Blakely General Store and Marina. Blakely is the sixth largest of the San Juans and you have to go around it when coming from Anacortes. Bounded by Thatcher Pass on the south and Peavine Pass on the north, Blakely creates a formidable barrier alongside Rosario Strait.

It is unique in that the entire island and the roads are private. We have been told that you must be a resident or guest to leave the General Store property and there are signs reinforcing the message. It doesn't matter what they are hiding or in truth protecting, our only interest is getting fuel at the long fuel dock and possibly an ice cream cone or donut.

The marina entrance might be a little shallow at low tide so watch yourself. Inside the well protected bay is a thirty plus boat moorage. They offer transient space and occasional evening barbecues.

Blakely's is very conveniently located for just about everyone coming and going, we make a point of stopping for fuel or just to sit on the lawn with the grazing deer and relaxing. If you are a boater camping at Spencer spit, James or Cypress, Blakely's may be your best bet for stocking up.

Blakely Island General Store and fuel dock is easy to get in and out from. - The water taxi from Anacortes is making a quick running stop.

# Lopez Island

Odlin Park - Spencer Spit Park - Fisherman Bay - Hummel Lake - Otis Perkins Park - Shark Reef Park
Agate Beach Park - Lopez Farm Cottage - Island Marine Center - Islander Resort

Lopez is number three of the big four, weighing in at almost thirty square miles which sounds puny so I did some conversion math and came up with 20,000 acres. Compare that to James Island at 113 acres and you see Lopez really is not puny at all.

Lopez is long and skinny and not nearly as hilly as Orcas so it makes sense it would have lots of farm and pasture land and be easier to bicycle. Over the years the islands two thousand plus residents have promoted being friendly and waving to everyone, everywhere. Now waving is an island tradition. Don't be surprised when someone looks up from their chores, smiles and waves. Bicycles, cars, boats, snoops, all get a wave, and you will soon be joining in. I hate to point, but on the other big three, cyclists are more likely to get a horn honk or worse. (Shaw Island is small, cars are few, so it doesn't really register on the wave/honk scale.)

The ferry landing at the far north end of Lopez is convenient if you're the ferry skipper, but the rest of us find it out at the end of nothing. So when you arrive, just start driving south on the only road, and after a few turns and four miles you will come to Lopez Village. Lopez Village is the only city and is the center of activity. Shops, grocery stores, museums, marinas, only in the village.

On the way to Lopez Village you will have chances to turn off and head for parks and resort like B&B's but I suggest for your first visit you head for Lopez Village and get acquainted with what it has to offer.

Sometimes there are more bicyclists getting off the ferry at Lopez than cars, and for good reason. Bicycling is great, many will spend the day riding and then catch the late ferry back to Friday Harbor. Why not, the ferry ride is free.

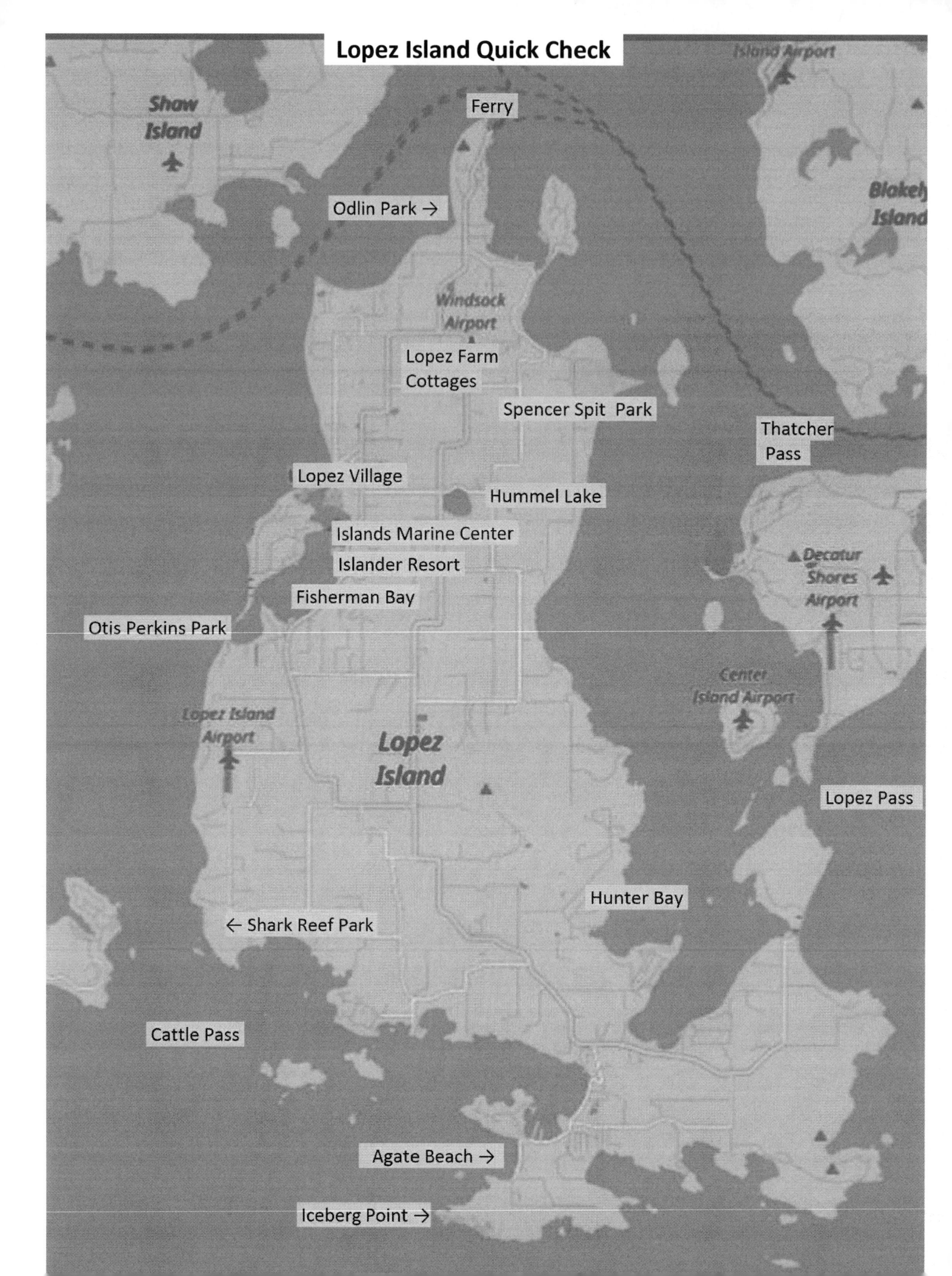

# Lopez Island Quick Check

**Lopez Island RV camp sites and campgrounds:**

1. Odlin County Park
2. Spencer Spit State Park
3. Lopez Farm Cottages
4. Lopez Islander Resort

**Lopez Island Parks:**

- Odlin County Park
- Spencer Spit State Park
- Hummel Park
- Otis Perkins Day use Park
- Shark Reef Park
- Agate Beach Park

**Resorts - Marinas:**

- Islands Marine Center
- Islander Resort
- Lopez Farm Cottages

**Anchorages**

- Fisherman Bay
- Odlin Park
- Spencer Spit
- Hunter Bay

**Lopez Island Transit stops**

Ferry Landing – Odlin Park – Lopez Farm Cottages – Lopez Village – Golf Course – Shark Reef Park – South End Gen. Store – Lopez School – Hummel Lake – Spencer Spit State Park – Lopez Village Market –

# Lopez Village

This is the Lopez Village Park and historic water tower. Chances are you will park near here or in the actual parking spaces adjacent and then walk around the area. Close by is a fudge shop, souvenir stores, crafty things, bakery, restaurant , the museum is next door,and a one block walk brings you to the island's two main grocery stores.

This park and bathroom are owned and operated 100% by the Lopez Island Chamber of commerce. It is not funded by the county or state, and yet they offer a **free restroom with free hot showers.** All you campers and boaters living out of your back packs and duffle bags take note, I said "FREE" They do like donations, and they certainly deserve your support.

I mentioned boaters and showers, you folks don't have to make that monthly cruise to Roche or Friday to get cleaned out of your quarters in a hurry, you can anchor off shore less than a baseball pitch from here, and dinghy over to the galvanized steel stairs – read on!

Every Saturday during the summer is the Lopez Farmers Market, right here in the village.

## For Boaters and Kayakers

I know kayakers are boaters – in the picture is a switchback public stairs that leads to the main street at Lopez Village. From the top of the stairs to the earlier mentioned free shower is about two hundred feet. You can also see the nice gravel dinghy/kayak beach. You can anchor out about a hundred feet.

It's extremely hard to spot things from offshore, but this place is easy. First head for the entrance to Fisherman Bay. Just outside the entrance is a red navigation aid (dolphin) on a piling It's the only one. Almost straight opposite the red nav. marker are the stairs. Careful when you anchor, departing skippers tend to pour on the coal right here, you will get waked and rocked.

🎯 Tip: I suggest you find a place to anchor inside Fisherman Bay and come back by dinghy, you don't have to shower, you can have breakfast or buy some fudge. For those of you spending the night at the Islander Resort or Islands Marine Center, taking the dinghy back here sure beats walking ¾ mile to town.

One last thing, the beach below the stairs is public, but the beach to the left and the right of the stairs is not. By now you should realize that Washington State allows private beach ownership, and in some instances even the tidelands are private. The best way to proceed is to assume everywhere is private except in parks and places marked public.

# Odlin County Park

*A*nother love hate relationship.  Love the location, love the facilities, but don't think much of the shallow beach.  Having a dock makes up for it though.  Love the warm sand and beach grass and hate rolling all night from passing wakes.  Love the fact that my daughter had reserved herself a waterfront camp site.

Odlin Park is an easy ten minute bike ride from the ferry terminal making it a perfect bike/hike or car camping destination.   Our family has used Odlin a number of times for meet ups – drop offs and even sleeping.

The 80 acre water front park features 30 camp sites,  9  of them on the beach and group camps back in the woods.  There are 4 anchor buoys offshore. They take reservations online  at http://www.sanjuanco.com/467/Reservations-Cancellations  When arriving on the ferry, follow the ferry road and turn right on Odlin Park Rd  one mile after rolling off the ferry.

Try -  http://www.sanjuanco.com/495/Lopez-Island  -    for the Odlin Park web site

In this image you can see six waterfront tent or RV sites. No boats are anchored or using any buoys. The dock is to the right outside the picture. The ferry heading for Friday Harbor is the one I just got off. Take note that three of the camp sites are open, this was a Wednesday, the third week in September. The weather was perfect and the crowds were gone. You can expect the same in May and June but you may be flirting with the weather.

TIP – If you are intent on making the most of your San Juan travels, utilizing boats, bicycles, cars and the ferry system to your advantage, you must use Odlin Park facilities and do some creative thinking outside the proverbial box. Odlin Park is the only place in the San Juans offering this unique combination of amenities. A dock - a campground - vehicle access - nearby ferry terminal and a nearly flat Island with hardly any traffic makes for almost unlimited excursion possibilities.

You can meet up - drop off - switch out - ride away - rendezvous - supply - provision - send home or trade out passengers - or just kick back and go for a long bike ride ending with a free shower in the village.

Let me me be clear – I like Odlin Park a lot, but not everything.  Sure it is centrally located in the San Juan's  making it very convenient for boating bicycling, and Lopez is hands down the best island for enjoying bike riding. The problem is sleeping on a boat.  If you look at a chart you will notice there are no prominent points to hide behind, so all boats going to and from Friday Harbor send their wakes at you.  I have anchored for and aft keeping the bow into the swells but when the wind doesn't cooperate, things get tippy, we dragged anchor once in a hopeless battle to outwit the elements.  Paying for a buoy won't stop wakes, and the dock has a two hour limit and will be just as rough, maybe worse.

Odlin County Park Dock

This little wharf and float is very handy, and under utilized by travelers. The fancy new concrete vault facility is only 250 feet away.  For dogs there's beach grass next to the dock.

I'll describe a few of our outings: We pulled in with the boat and unloaded bikes and gear, and then anchored about where the above picture was taken.  I then ran back with the dinghy and dragged it onto the float for safe keeping.  We then, without any worries rode into Lopez Village (twenty minutes) and on around the island. Another time we dropped off our kids and their bikes and they caught the ferry to Friday Harbor that night. And yet another time we dropped people off and picked them up two days later.

This is the only place in the San Juans that offers this combination of boater/vehicle and camping access.  You are well advised to plan creative outings utilizing Odlin Park.

# Spencer Spit State Park

Judging by the name, one would expect this park to have a history where someone named Spencer played a significant role. Right you are. The Spencer family lived on the property for fifty years before selling it to the State, apparently the name stuck. Out on the end of the namesake spit is a replica of the Spencer log cabin.

My guess is that it was a summer place because wind and storms and low exposed spits are bad combinations. I've looked for some supporting research but haven't found any.

This is the only state park on Lopez that you can drive to. When you are on the ferry you go by Frost Island which partially blocks your view of the spit but Frost Island also protects it from wakes. Spencer Spit Park has Cascadia Marine Trail camp sites for kayakers. Group sites, hiker biker sites, and of course car campers make up the majority of the fifty or so private camping spots. The grounds cover 138 acres so you know there are lots of thick woods and trails. There is a summer time concessionaire that rents bicycles for use to ride around the island. Many boaters will anchor offshore in the lee of the spit or hook onto one of the eleven buoys, and come ashore by dinghy to rent bicycles for a day of exploring. We have brought our bikes ashore in the dinghy which is difficult primarily because of the substantial distance pushing them through sand, gravel and trail before getting to anything paved. Being doable but a pain reinforces my contention that Odlin Park is best for getting bikes from boat to shore. Here is the web site for making reservations and learning more about Spencer Spit http://parks.state.wa.us/687/Spencer-Spit

The park is only 3 ½ miles from the ferry and then doubling back some, only 2 ½ miles to Lopez Village. These short distances make bicycle camping a favorite on Lopez.

This is Spencer Spit and that is a parks building up close. Way down at the far end of the spit is the Spencer Cabin. The spit ends before Frost Island leaving a narrow but deep channel you can run your boat through. When the wind blows here, and my experience is that it always blows here, you can anchor in the lee of the spit for flat water. The long walk to the park bathrooms after a windy dinghy ride makes this place low on my list, but in the summer it is normal to see thirty boats here. Honestly, I don't get it!

Spencer Cabin

# Lopez Farm Cottages and Tent Camping

All the tent and glamping sites on Lopez are at the north end of the Island within a few miles of each other, the ferry landing and Lopez Village. Lopez Farm Cottages are right on the main road on the way to the Village.

They have a woodsy setting with open meadows, promising serenity, peace and quiet. In fact they promote on their web site a few things you should note that may influence your decision to visit.

- No Children under 14
- No RV's
- No loud electronics (in my day it was called a boom box)
- No pets.
- Minimal vehicle intrusion (headlights, engine noise)

Their stated goal is for guest serenity, with facilities primarily aimed at singles and couples.

If you find yourself drawn to wine tasting, bicycling, relaxing, you should consider reserving a date.

They have fifteen premium tent sites and five cabins a hot shower house, hot tub, plus picnic and cooking buildings coupled with bicycle rentals make Lopez Farm Cottages a destination to think about.

Lastly, since San Juan Transit makes regular stops, you can visit here without a car or bicycle.

# Hummel Lake

$\mathcal{H}$ummel Lake is a strange little lake, and neat at the same time. It feels square shaped when you drive or bike along side of it, mostly because the road comes to a four way stop with the lake on both roads. Right at the stop sign is a small gravel parking lot with a single stall toilet and a life jacket lending shed that resembles a fruit stand. There's a short little beach and trail from the parking lot made by years of people trampling the vegetation, around the edges are miscellaneous skiffs and beat up canoes shoved into the bushes. Scattered around are half a dozen ratty looking folding camp chairs.

My description should conjure up images of a fishing hole frequented by local Huck Finns and grisly retired pioneer islanders chasing catfish. That's the strange part of Hummel Lake, the neat part is down Center Road a quarter mile where the forest begins. A paved driveway leads quietly through a shady woods to a small parking lot. Nestled nearby is a modern concrete restroom and a single trail. The trail leads a circuitous route deeper into the forest and then turns at an open grassy field before continuing on a meandering mazelike journey.

Well placed memorial benches beckon me to remove a pebble from my shoe before moving on.

*At the end of the trail is serene Hummel Lake, I can see the fish camp, but a quarter mile blurs the memory, it may as well be ten.* The wood planked walkway stretches across swamp and lilies, guiding me to a small float. Water grasses and cattails wave, towering four feet over my head, first I hear, then glimpse water birds fleeing my clomping approach.

Find Hummel Lake Preserve where Center Rd crosses Hummel Lake Rd

# Shark Reef Sanctuary

Continuing on Center Road, which really does run down the center of the island, there are no turns and the hill is slight. I continue straight as an arrow. Today we are in the car, lunch from the village market is on the console between us. Last time, two years earlier I was riding my bicycle, the same hill was not a struggle but made me wonder how far I would go before turning around. We turn right on Fisherman Bay Rd, go straight at the turn on Davis Bay Rd, one right angle corner and another arrow straight section to Burt Rd. Burt Rd ends at a tee intersection, I'm lost. I don't have a map. There are no street signs. I ask a bike rider where he came from and what was down that direction, he said he didn't know. Thanks I said. I turned left for no reason and in a quarter mile parked in a wooded area by a sign that said Shark Reef Sanctuary.

My advice to everyone is, if you are driving a car, it's probably ok to wander around, after all, how lost can you get in only thirty square miles. If you are riding a bicycle, wasting energy and burning daylight, get a map.

I see more cars bicycles and people than I have seen in the last hour. They are all hanging around the parking lot and deserted country road. Its not tall forest like at Hummel Lake, it's thick shore pine and salal as high as my shoulders, to me that means the ocean is near. The trail dives right in, we pass a bathroom and some other hikers. Soon I hear roaring rapids, I know the unmistakable sound of a mountain cascade. This is wrong, I should be hearing surf and gulls, not river rapids. The noise is deafening as we close in. We still can't see anything but the trail, and then it's gets brighter as the scruffy trees give way to blue sky.

We walk out onto some boulders and brace ourselves, there is no beach, no trail, in front of us is Shark Reef, beyond is Cattle Pass, across the pass is Cattle Point and Cattle Point Light.

I'm in awe, the pass is at full ebb, the inner San Juans are draining themselves as fast as the moon, the sun, and earths gravity pulls the rushing water out Cattle Pass. The noise is coming from everywhere, and everywhere is white water. My mind wanders and then remembers our sloop Mariah. The kids were little, we came through the other direction on a full flood. Funny though, I don't remember the roar, just the speed we flew that half mile.

It would be a mistake to visit by boat, but I highly recommend hiking in. It's day use only.

# Agate Beach County Park

Agates are everywhere, but to get a beach named Agate Beach there must be more than normal, at least that's what I think.

The park is a day use county park with a couple picnic tables set in a grass parking area. Across the street is a short stairway leading to the beach.

Agate Beach Park is in a cove fronting on the Strait of Juan De Fuca pretty much at the end of the road.

As you can see in the lower picture, private property is clearly marked behind sign.

## Iceberg point

The Agate Beach parking lot is also used for those hiking the trail to Iceberg Point.

I regret I have not hiked the Iceberg Point trail so I don't have first hand knowledge. But I have read very exciting good things about it and look forward to making the journey asap.

Below is an excerpt from the BLM

Iceberg Point is located on the southwest tip of Lopez Island. Drive south on Mud Bay Road. Turn Right on Mackaye Harbor road to the County Park at Agate Beach. Park at Agate Beach, County Park, Day-use area. Hike south along the Mackaye Harbor road past where the "End of County Road" signs are posted. At this point you will be entering private land- Please be respectful of the property-. Turn Right at the driveway with a green metal gate. Hike around this gate on the right side, and then left at the fork in the road behind the next gate. Follow this trail for about 1/2 mile to access BLM lands

## Mackaye Harbor Boat Launch

*I*f you are driving around the San Juans looking for neat places, it doesn't take long to realize that either they don't believe in signs, or they want to keep things secret. Or maybe I'm just not as quick as the targeted sign reader.

The south end of Lopez Island is a kayakers paradise. Bays, little coves, headlands and remoteness, coupled with nasty currents and the Strait of Juan De Fuca separate recreational boaters from the more adventuress of us. That being said, it makes no sense, nor is it practical to paddle all the way from one of the north end launch spots.

Mackaye Harbor public ramp has free parking and a dock, although the dock is not next to the ramp making bigger boat launching a wet to the waist proposition. (Not me, I won't launch without a float) Kayakers will find it perfectly acceptable since they don't need a ramp – parking and a bathroom suffices.

Directions: Head south on Fisherman Bay Rd or Center Rd. Follow Center to Mud Bay Rd, turn right on Mackaye Harbor Rd, turn right on Norman Rd, follow to end.

All boaters know to have a chart, all car drivers should know to bring a map. This guidebook in spite of its name is not a book of maps. Please don't rely on my lame directions to find your way around.

## Hunter Bay County Dock and Boat Ramp

*H*unter Bay is at the end of Islandale Rd, follow Mud Bay Rd and turn left on Islandale. There is a ramp a float, free parking and a portable bathroom.

Hunter Bay and Mud Bay are next to each other and very protected, you wont find scary waves here like you may at Mackaye Harbor and Agate Beach. The difference is due to being off the Strait of Juan de Fuca versus Lopez Sound. You can paddle over to Lopez Pass and into Rosario Strait if you are inclined, but Hunter and Mud Bays offer great scenery for recreational paddlers desiring flat water.

## Southend General Store and Restaurant

*O*nce you leave civilization behind and head to the south end of Lopez Island, you will probably wish you had something. Wine or gas come to mind? They are open year round with off season hours and are right on Mud Bay Rd. If you are heading to Agate Beach or Mackaye Harbor you will miss them. Stay on Mud Bay a little longer. f you happen to be anchored, or at the Hunter Bay Dock, it's a short one mile bike ride.

# Otis Perkins Day Park

Locally referred to as "the spit" you have probably seen it when you gazed across Fisherman Bay wondering where those houses get access, well now you know. They drive on a low narrow isthmus that looks like a good one-day winter storm will make them an island for sure. To get to Otis Perkins Park simply head south from the Village on Fisherman Bay Rd and turn right on the first road, that's Bayshore road, follow to the park. The park is not at the end of the road but occupy's the narrowest part of "the spit" for a about a quarter mile. There is a small parking lot and a picnic table facing Lopez sound, and of course the ever present no trespassing sign warning wandering beachcombers not to go south on the beach, north is approved, so you will have about a quarter mile of beachcombing to look forward to, a rarity in the San Juans for sure.

Of the many islands in the San Juans, only 172 have names

# Islands Marine Center

*F*irst – notice in the picture that the tide is out (think down) and yet the boats are still floating, however some of them can't leave because all of Fisherman Bay is shallow and at the entrance there may be only three feet of water. Sometimes it is best to stay put until things begin to improve.

🎯 Tip: Always leave on a rising tide if you suspect depth issues, that way if you run aground you will soon float free. On a falling tide you will soon be in big trouble.

The walk into the village is ¾ of a mile, I don't make it anymore, I take the dinghy. See the "for boaters and kayakers" at the start of the Lopez section.

The below info is from the Lopez Chamber.

VHF channel 69. Located on Fisherman Bay. Full-service marina facility: 100-slip marina, factory-authorized service dept., Haul outs, fully-stocked chandlery, marine & auto parts dept., sales of Ocean Sport and Pursuit. Ice, licenses, bait and tackle; apartment rentals. Mon-Sat 8:30am to 5pm. July-Aug 8:30am to 6pm.

2793 Fisherman Bay Road

(360) 468-3377   Fax: (360) 468-2283

# Lopez Islander Resort Marina

The Islander has been the "go to" marine resort for years. People have told me they arrive by boat or car and have no reason to leave. They have tent sites and RV sites but do not have RV hook ups. They also rent cabins. They ask for guests to make reservations. They are next door to Islands Marine center which means its a ¾ mile hike into Lopez Village. The below info is from the Lopez Chamber.

VHF Channel 78A. Located on charming Fisherman Bay. Overnight guest moorage and restaurant moorage available daily. Dock store, ice and bait, fuel, propane, laundry, new pool, new Jacuzzi, new showers & restrooms, kayaks, bicycles, on-island bakery, free WI-FI in lodge, grocery & liquor store, golf and tennis. Islander Waterfront Restaurant & deck dining overlooking Fisherman Bay, serving Northwest cuisine and Tiki Cocktail Lounge featuring live music and dancing. New workout facilities available.

2864 Fisherman Bay Road

(360) 468-2233    Toll Free: (800) 736-3434    For more information, visit www.lopezfun.com

# Shaw Island

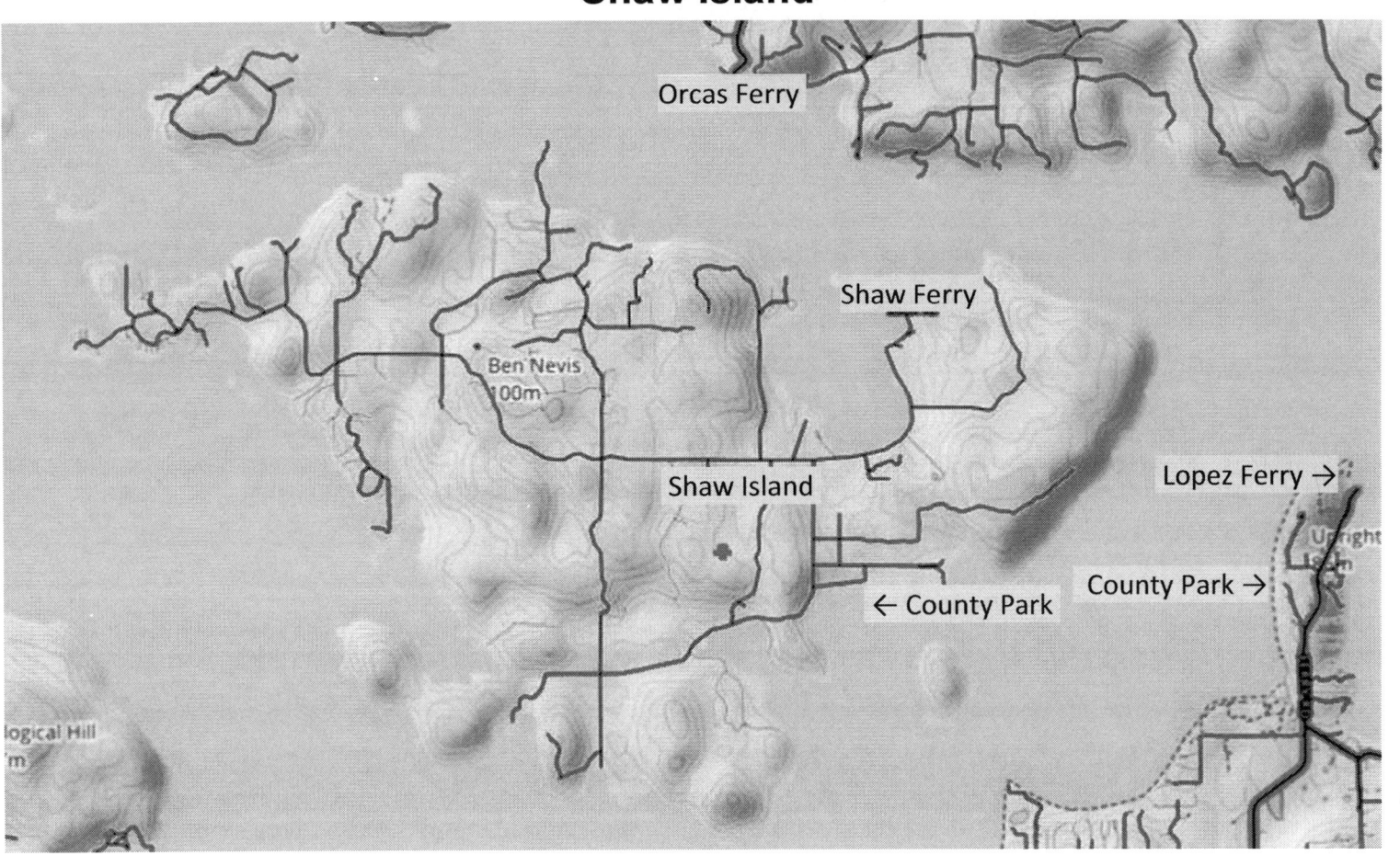

When you look at large maps you notice that Shaw Island is right in the middle of the San Juan Islands. You would think that the island would become the center of activity but the opposite is true. Shaw is rural with next to nothing in the way of development. Around 175 residents call Shaw home. To put that number in perspective, the ferry serving Shaw could transport the entire population and their cars in a single run and still have room for regular traffic. At the ferry landing is a small older structure housing a seasonal store that was operated for more than thirty years by nuns. Down on the water behind the store is a small dock. If you arrive by private boat, it may be hard to spot the float because the ferry terminal tends to overwhelm the view. There are no *"welcome,"* or *"come up to the store signs,"* From conversations I have had with the store clerk they rent overnight space but it is very limited. You may have to raft or tie up creatively in thin water while you run up the gangway.

At the top of the ferry ramp across from the store is this cute little park where you can picnic while you wait for the ferry.

141

The "all weather" Shaw Island community bulletin board and mail box is steps from the ferry. Island life, events and general news is posted by everyone for all to read. It's kind of like a chat room or forum without a password, spell check, or usb port.

One and a half miles from the ferry is Shaw County Park. The campground offers ten or eleven sites with one shared site for those without a car (biker/kayaker) Even though this is a waterfront park all the campsites are above a steep bank, private and woodsy without easy access to the beach. Everyone has to walk over to the community stairs or boat ramp.

The picture below is of the picnic shelter and fireplace., It would be welcome in a storm, that's for sure. This is a popular place and during the summer reservations are smart. All the county parks use the same web site for reservations - They start taking reservations for all the parks in March - http://sanjuanco.com/466/Camping-Information

The store closes from mid September until May. Shaw Park has reduced rates in the winter and stays open on a first come basis. There are no other parks, stores or public beach access on Shaw.

**Boaters anchored in Blind Bay** need to know that there is no shore access by landing your dinghy or kayak. Getting to that enticing looking county road circling much of Blind Bay would require a boater to land on posted private beach and trespass. Besides that the shore is not dinghy friendly and there is nowhere to go once you get there.

I suggest that visitors to Shaw arrive as a car or kayak camper heading for Shaw Park, or come by ferry with a bicycle intending to ride around the island and then catch a later ferry back to another island where they are camping. We have caught the 8:30 ferry departing Friday and returned to Friday on the 1:30 ferry. It's simple (not too early) and free, how can that be anything but a great excursion?

# Victoria and Butchart Gardens

Visiting Canada does not need to complicate your travels, but you do need to set aside a little time If it is to be part of a San Juan trip. Car travelers have several considerations, first off, you must decide if you are going to travel in a great circle or simply over and back. I have done both and now leave the car behind. Keep reading and I will explain our evolution and simplified itinerary's.

**For this typical visit** lets begin in Port Angeles, taking our car and boarding the MV Coho ferry (Black Ball Lines) landing in Victoria about ninety minutes later. In your planning you need to set aside about three hours for loading, unloading and going through customs, and it could be more. You also must have reservations in the summer season or you risk not making the departure you plan. Fares are about $65 for the car and driver and about $20 for each passenger - one way - you pay again coming back. People on foot hauling a bicycle or kayak pay another $6.50. The MV Coho sails several times daily so you have some planning options, but you will have 3 - 6 hours tied up both ways no matter what.

You're in Victoria, you don't need a car so park it and walk around, check in at a local hotel downtown, or get a motel in the outskirts. You can do a whirlwind tour of downtown, and then drive to Butchart Gardens, afterwards head for Goldstream Provincial Campground only 12 miles away.

**Tomorrow, or in a few days** you will catch the Washington State ferry in Sidney. Sidney is about fifteen miles north of Victoria. This is the ferry that goes through the San Juans landing in Anacortes. The rates are about the same as the Black Ball Lines rates. You can get off at Friday Harbor and finish your vacation in the San Juans continuing on to Anacortes days or weeks later. There is only one Canada to Anacortes ferry each way each day through the San Juan's so you must plan your schedule accordingly.

**As an alternative**, you can reverse the route beginning in Anacortes with stop overs in the islands, and finish in Port Angeles for about the same amount of convenience and fun times.

Ok, that was a typical trip scenario. I recommend you find a all day parking spot in Victoria and walk around the downtown area checking out the many blocks of touristy shops. Stroll through the Empress Hotel, even stop for tea if the ambience suits you. Plan a three hour visit to the Royal BC Museum next door and lastly ride a double decker bus out to Butchart Gardens. Even though you have your car parked nearby you should still ride the bus. The driver gives a mini tour of Victoria on the way plus offers to guide you through the gardens. The guided tour alone is worth the price – and he wont get lost and you will. There is more to see in Victoria, and it is all easy walking. Thunderbird Park (Totem Pole Park) the government building.

**That's the way we used to do it – Lets move on to what we do today.**

We learned many years ago that bringing our car to Victoria was an expensive pain in the you know, and even with young kids we were much better off leaving the car in free parking in Port Angeles and traveling as foot passengers. Foot passengers are first on, first off, and will be inside eating breakfast while cars are still loading. In Victoria you can be walking into the Empress before the first car unloads.

**Here is a quickie run down of what we do now.**

We start out by camping near Port Angeles at Heart O' the Hills campground, only 7 miles from the ferry terminal. You could motel it. We set up camp the afternoon before. In the morning we leave camp set up ready for our late return and take the car to the ferry where we park a few blocks away for free parking. **We board as foot passengers**, bypassing all the folks in their cars at both ends, and spend the day in Victoria taking the last ferry back that evening. The time and hassle savings by leaving the car behind is great and the Butchart Gardens tour bus drivers, time their arrival back at the ferry terminal to catch the ferry. It is an easy one day visit hitting the hot spots with time to spare. When you get back to camp you will be ready to hit the sack, and the kids will already be asleep.

A major consideration is that we **don't go to the San Juans and Victoria on the same trip**. A more relaxed trip will happen if you rent a room in Victoria for one night, carrying backpacks, but still leaving your car in Port Angeles. We did exactly that one trip and that allowed us to depart later and come back earlier making for a low key outstanding visit.

# Quick Check
## Victoria - Butchart Gardens - Sidney Spit Park - Sidney - Roche Harbor

Going by boat to be a tourist in Victoria is an excellent decision putting you right downtown. Everything is an easy walk from the inner harbor where you will berth directly in front of the Empress Hotel.

The restrooms are at the end of the esplanade. Harbormaster aides will come to register you at your boat. All you need to do is grab a spot after checking in with customs around the corner at the red dock. (They may have changed check in to an 800 phone call.)

Part of the thrill of going to Victoria is docking at the seawall marina right in front of the Empress hotel. Street minstrels and mimes will entertain you. Everything to see is at your swimstep.

When you depart, fuel is readily available on your way out of the inner harbor.

Keep to one side, you are sharing the water with seaplanes.

Butchart Gardens, Wow. Indescribable as a destination. You need to come here if you like flowers. There are five free buoys talking distance from the dinghy dock where you will pay to get in. If you can't get a buoy just motor around the corner and anchor anywhere you want in a long still bay (Tod Inlet) and paddle back to the dinghy dock. We like to walk the gardens late in the afternoon, then wait for the sun to set and walk again under the lights. I recommend you do the same. Then head for the boat for dinner and bed on the smoothest calmest inlet you have ever seen.

🎯 Tip: on Saturday nights all summer they shoot off fireworks, you can sit on the lawn for a front seat or park your boat just right, for a sneak peak through the trees.

This fountain dances to colored lights and music.

You are looking at the back door boater entrance to Butchart Gardens. Once you get anchored, simply dinghy over to the dock pay your entrance fees and you are all set. Second day tickets are heavily discounted.

This is the same dinghy dock, making it the longest I have ever seen. The free buoys in the background get grabbed quick but you can anchor very close, so don't worry about not getting a buoy.

Coming over here is a snap, use Roche Harbor or Stuart for your jump off point, try to cross Haro Strait near slack water. It is ten miles to Sidney Marina where you must check in, and then its another thirteen miles around Saanich Peninsula to Tod Inlet.

Sometimes on the way back, the weather and seas conspire to close you out. If you need to, simply head for Sidney Spit Park and wait it out. Sidney Spit Park has otters, deer and lots of purple martins. The dock boasts tie up space and in the shallow bay are rows of buoys, or you may anchor for free. Canadians from Sidney use the park for day-use, riding a seasonal shuttle back and forth or spending the night camping in the 27 site walk in campground. On shore are miles of level open trails with herds of deer wandering about. The island park has resident rangers , well kept picnic shelters and restroom facilities. Wheelbarrows are provided making overnight stays on shore easy.

When you arrive back in the USA, you must check in first before you land anywhere else. This means you can not run to Stuart Island for the night and check in later. The easiest system is to go straight back to Roche Harbor and present yourself at the red customs dock along with your passports. You will be asked to declare your taxable purchases, and then you are free to roam.

# Vancouver BC for Boaters

Vancouver British Columbia is forty miles north of Bellingham, it is also forty miles north of Sucia by boat. Somewhere I said I won't sugar coat anything, but I will rave where appropriate. Well – Vancouver's Granville Island district is worth raving about.

We weren't planning to spend any time there, just check in and get back out in the Strait of Georgia was the plan. We departed Patos Island early about 6 am because I wanted to get a long way up the Sunshine Coast towards Princess Louisa Inlet. Maybe I should have paid more attention to the weather. Eight foot broadsides slammed us for three of our eight hour run to False Creek. At times I was pushing all the rpm the old diesel could muster just to keep her pointed more or less the right direction. We were dangerously low on Dramamine and thoroughly beat up when we rounded the corner at English Bay and idled into tranquil False Creek. What a relief, I knew we would not be leaving anytime soon.

We found the old customs check in dock easy enough only to read a sign saying to call an 800 number. The rest was an easy handful of questions and I had my approval entry number taped to the window. Further inside False Creek, (which is really a short narrow bay) we swung over to a floating visitor center to talk with the *visiting-boater-greeter* fellow that gave us tourist brochures and answered our questions. Soon we anchored and headed for the dinghy dock at **Granville Island Public Market** for unwinding and dinner.

Locals tout Granville Island as the reigning King of Vancouver destinations – and the Public Market as the crown jewel of indoor Farmers Markets, rivaling all others. I don't disagree, plus they are open every day. Venders with jewelry, ceramics, fused glass, exotic foods, fashion accessories jam the place. The list is truly endless - a doggy bakery, street performers, micro breweries…. They change venders regularly to assure new, fresh and quality shopping.

## False Creek

False creek is a 1 ½ mile long narrow bay. Too wide to yell across but you can certainly wave. The entire bay is ringed with a level paved bike and pedestrian path. Aqua Bus stops are conveniently spaced to give quick access to False creeks many waterfront condos and businesses. At any given time there may be five to ten Aqua Buses darting between stops keeping a tight fifteen minute or less schedule. False Creek abuts World famous Stanley Park and Lions Gate suspension bridge creating a 10 mile circular bike path that winds through forest, park, and some of Vancouver's most exclusive high rise towers. You are welcome to anchor and enjoy the city. Everyone you meet smiles and is genuinely friendly - we're going back.

### Tip

I highly recommend you consider making False Creek your primary destination – not just a place to check in, but a place to spend some time. You won't regret it.

False Creek and Granville Island Market is not just for tourists, the shore is lined with local bad boys and soaring condos. See the tiny Aquabus at the stop in front of this one hundred and seventy five footer.

This is the Aquabus stop at Sunset Beach that serves Stanley Park. We chose to ride our bikes from the Public Market all the way around Stanley Park, under Lions Gate Bridge to Coal Harbor, and then on around all of False Creek. It was a ten mile level ride that gave us a wonderful half day tour of Vancouver.

When you come back stateside you must check in first. Anacortes, Friday Harbor, Roche Harbor, Bellingham, are all check in places but going to Point Roberts is undoubtedly closest and most convenient, especially if you plan more stops in the San Juan's.

Point Roberts Marina is easy to find, its on the tip of the peninsula extending south just past the Tsawwassen Ferry terminal. Once inside the marina tie up at the first dock on the right. After checking in you can stay at Point Roberts or head for Patos or Sucia, and the San Juans twelve miles further south.

# Customs and Canada for Boaters only

## Dealing with Customs

**This little snippet is a reprint from our 2014 Cruise guide - since then we have entered Canada two more times - the info. is still valid**

If you plan to leave the area and run across to Canada there will be a few things to consider. First off, do not use this guide or any other as your last up to date source of information. Over the years border crossing procedures have changed. Interestingly, reports of difficulty at vehicle points of entry seem to be much more prevalent than at cruising points of entry. Perhaps cruisers are more likable. Do yourself a favor and check for new rules before you go. A simple web search and phone call may be all that's needed. This is the web site where U.S. information and phone numbers are found for Customs and checking in at Ports of Entry. https://www.cbp.gov/travel/pleasure-boats-private-flyers/pleasure-boat-overview

The following is my take and experience as of our crossings in 2012 -2014- 2015. You may drive your boat through Canadian waters past their islands on your way somewhere, but you can't land. Before you may go ashore, you must check in. For our purposes the check in places are at Victoria or Sidney, or False Creek in Vancouver. Upon arrival (24/7) at the customs dock you will find a phone on a pole and nothing else. (2017 update - look for a sign with an 800 number) There is no office, just a phone. Have a piece of paper and a pencil handy, then just pick up the receiver and say hello. A friendly voice will want to know your names, ages, and boat type, name, age and number. They may ask where you're going and for how long. That's it, they will give you a number, write it down and tape it to your window so it's visible from the dock wherever you tie up. Now that your checked in you may go anywhere you want, just remember to plan your visit around checking in before you go anywhere else. When you leave Canada, just go. There is no checking out required for either country.

Coming back to the states is a little more serious. Just like Canada you may not touch anything until you check in. This makes trip planning more difficult because running to Roche or Bellingham may be out of your way. You are not allowed to spend the night at Stuart or Sucia and then check in the next morning, you must check in first, then back track to where you really want to go. At Roche Harbor simply tie up at the red painted customs dock out on the end, you can't miss it. Everyone must stay on the boat, they are not allowed to run up the float to use the bathroom until later. One person from your boat must walk into the office on the float and present your passports and identification for everyone on board. They will ask similar questions to what the Canadians asked and they will want that Canadian number so don't lose it. Fresh fruits seems to be an issue so we try not to bring any back. Canned and sealed food stuffs are no problem. We have never had our boats searched or any issues except once when I made a joke that failed to bring a smile or even a hint of friendliness. Children need identification, but not passports. (this may change or have an age requirement, and is one thing I would definitely find out) Adults need passports, and you can apply for them at your post office. Plan ahead, passports may take several months to arrive.

If it is a busy sunny weekend there will be other boats circling and waiting for your space at the red dock so you must move along and find another place to dawdle or dally about after check in.

Now you may go to the restroom.

## Pump Out Locations

When you have to go and nowhere to go. Many of the listed places are written about in the guidebook. Most are free but some charge a fee. If an attendant helps they will appreciate being tipped.

It is illegal to dump your tanks anywhere in the San Juan's and I think you should assume the same for Canadian waters too.

| | | |
|---|---|---|
| Cap Sante - Anacortes | Deer Harbor - Orcas | Bellingham Cruise Term. |
| Squalicum Harbor - Bellingham | La Conner Marina - La Conner | Friday Harbor |
| Islands Marine Center - Lopez | Marine Ser. Ctr. - Anacortes | Reid Harbor - Stuart Island |
| Blain Harbor Marina - Blaine | Shelter Bay - La Conner | Roche Harbor - San Juan |
| Cornet Bay - Deception Pass | Point Roberts Marina | Skyline Marina - Anacortes |

## Larger Anchorages

When you are from out of town without local knowledge, it is not easy to just pull up and drop your anchor any old place. When it is getting dark and you are running out of options, it is a hundred times tougher. This list of suitable places and brief location hints may help you out one day. These are mostly large places where you wont bother or be bothered, and you can probably show up in the dark and get hooked without much problem, but I would avoid like a jagged reef, intentionally letting darkness over take you without a place to go or action plan.

| | | |
|---|---|---|
| Blind Bay - Shaw Is. | Indian Cove - Shaw Is. | Bowman Bay - Deception Pass |
| Park Bay - Shaw Is. | Roche Harbor | Shoal Bay - Lopez north |
| Fisherman Bay - Lopez | Friday Harbor | Deepwater Bay - Cypress south |
| Echo Bay- Fossil Bay - Sucia | Reid & Prevost Hbrs - Stuart Is. | Saddle bag Island Park |
| Judd Bay - Eastsound - Orcas | Griffin Bay by American Camp | Cornet Bay - Deception Pass |
| Garrisson Bay - San Juan | Spencer Spit - Lopez | Hope Island - north side |
| Inati Bay - Lummi Is. | Hunter Bay - Lopez south | |

This is not a list of cool nooks and parks. I don't want anyone pinning hopes on an already filled up location so I didn't list any small places where all the anchor spots may be taken and you won't be welcome swinging into people already anchored. Eagle Harbor and James Island are good examples of where you may not find happiness showing up after dark. ***This list is more of a last chance, "I can't go on, please let me find a spot to sleep kind of list."***

Tip: don't put yourself and your crew in this kind of situation – especially when on vacation.

# Fuel and Grocery Stores on the Water

Boat fuel is readily available, (gas or diesel) and at mostly reasonable prices. You should not expect late hours or boat services at fuel docks. Remember 1/3 out 1/3 to get back and 1/3 for reserve just in case.

Tip 🎯 *I fill my tanks when I can, not just when I need it.*

1. **Anacortes:** (Cap Sante)
2. **La Conner** on Swinomish Channel
3. **Cornet Bay** Marina at Deception Pass
4. **Squalicum Harbor** in Bellingham
5. **Blakelys** at Peavine Pass on Blakely Island
6. **West Beach Resort** on north side of Orcas
7. **Fisherman Bay** on Lopez Island
8. **Friday Harbor:** San Juan Island
9. **Roche Harbor:** San Juan Island
10. **Deer Harbor** Orcas Island
11. **Rosario Resort** Orcas Island

**Anacortes** (Cap Sante)
Fuel dock is in front of main office and Safeway is across the street, but you will be asked to move away from fuel dock after fueling while you run for provisions.
(360) 293-0694. For fuel and slip assignments or (Harbor Master) VHF #66

**La Conner** on Swinomish Channel:
The fuel dock is at the north end of town and they have a very small selection in the store, but if you move south after fueling about a 1/4 mile and tie up at one of the three public floats you can walk one block to the main store in La Conner (Pioneer market) where they have everything you could want, including ice and wine. The floats at the seawall are self serve with a pay kiosk at the top of the gangplanks. Public bathrooms are very close on the main street. (We like La Conner a lot)
Harbor Master and office at marina 360-466-3118    VHF #66

**Cornet Bay** Marina at Deception Pass:
For groceries only, tie up at the State Park floats and walk 1/4 mile to a small convenience store or take boat right to fuel dock at next facility over and save the walk. (360) 675-5411

**Squalicum Harbor** in Bellingham:
Fuel dock and transient moorage, but groceries are a healthy walk. We have been told, they run a shuttle during the day time, but we always find a car or bike it.. Bellingham is a major city and has anything you need. Harbor Master – VHF # 16 or (360) 676-2542

**Blakelys** at Peavine Pass on Blake Island:
Easy and convenient fuel and small grocery store with deli counter. Plenty of room at the float and no rush, we sit on the lawn and eat ice cream each time we stop by..
General store and Marina Harbor Master, (360) 375-6121

**West beach resort** on north side of Orcas near Sucia:
Easy and handy if your at Sucia or taking the northern route around Orcas.
Fuel dock and general grocery store with deli.
(watch your draft at low tide)   (877)937-8224

**Fisherman Bay** on Lopez Island:
Islander Resort and Marina, fuel and store - Harbor Master (360) 468-2233
Watch your draft at entrance to bay at low tide.

**Friday Harbor:** San Juan Island:
Fuel dock, short walk to large grocery store  (Kings) on main street
360-378-2688  or call Harbor Master on #66 for slips

**Roche Harbor:** San Juan Island:
Fuel dock, well stocked grocery store right at top of gang plank, restaurants,
Slip assignment  800.586.3590  or Harbor Master vhf #78

**Deer Harbor** Orcas Island
Fuel dock, small store and deli out on dock, transient moorage  – county dock adjacent to fuel dock
(360) 376-3037

**Rosario Resort** Orcas Island:
Fuel dock, store and restaurant, just a short walk, you can leave boat at float while you shop and dine.
(360) 376-2222   Harbor Master vhf #78  or 360-376-2152

## *Fuel tips just for Boaters*

Tip: You need to manage your fuel consumption and how much fuel you carry. If you are new to boating you may mistakenly treat your boat like you do your car. (I'll have a bucks worth of premium please) You can't walk to the gas station or call for a delivery without a huge expense, and running out somewhere may be  life threatening.  Deciding to cross a strait or run a long distance with barely enough fuel is a beginners mistake.

When the wind (waves) or current catches you by surprise, your planned fuel consumption goes out the window, your two gallon per hour rate goes to ten gallons, and your planned one hour crossing becomes five, or worse, and then you end up not where you planned.

It is quite acceptable to carry extra portable tanks on deck, (not in the cabin or in an un-vented locker) just remember to secure them, keep fumes out of the bilge, and have a way to safely transfer fuel to your operating tank.

Tip: *I can't stress the importance of the last tip enough*, but as they say you can't fix dumb.

Tip:  Just a thought for you to remember;  Several times at fuel stops I have been told by the operator that they will wait a little after closing if I call and tell them I'm on my way.  The numbers listed, will go to the office or harbor master.  You will need to ask for the fuel dock or number.

# *Launching Ramps*

Squalicum Harbor in Bellingham is by far the best ramp and facility around, and has my highest recommendation. If your planning to go to Sucia for the first night, Squalicum Harbor is the closest.

**Squalicum Harbor**   Tip: this is where you want to go.
- Four lanes, suitable at all tide levels, open 24/7
- Lots of free parking, long or short term (this is a $100+ savings per week)
- Fresh water wash down hoses (always rinse your trailer immediately after immersion, don't wait until you return a week later.)
- On site restaurants, and bathrooms with showers.
- Transient boat docks for overnight visits
- Major stores near by, but not walking distance
- Closest jump off point to Sucia, Matia and Patos Islands
- Fuel dock, pump out

*Next on the list of popular launching points is*

**Cap Sante in Anacortes**

- Two sling launches (big and little) but no ramp (keeping your trailer out of salt water is a good thing) may require reservation or waiting in line, not 24/7 use
- Fee parking, long term, short term (RV parking too) fees add up fast
- Restaurants, bathrooms, showers
- Transient boat docks for overnight visits
- A few major stores near by (short walk)
- Fuel dock, pump out
- Closest to Friday Harbor and inner island area

*Not very far, but overlooked is*

**La Conner on the Swinomish Channel**

- Big and little travel lifts (slings) at several marinas (will need reservations)
- One lane city ramp with float, 24/7 use, all tides except minus (under Rainbow Bridge)
- Inexpensive, limited parking at ramp but lots of pay parking at marinas
- Transient docks for overnights at marina and along city seawall (really nice stopover place for lunch or the night at three city floats)
- Restaurants, quite a few, all walking distance
- No national stores but a very well stocked local store is a short walk
- Fuel and pump outs
- Closest to Deception Pass and heading south to Puget Sound area

*Best kept secret is*

## Cornet Bay at Deception Pass State Park

Cornet Bay is my second ramp choice, and I use it if my plans call for easy access to the southern area, and most importantly long term hassle free parking and 24/7 usage. (daily fee) Excellent choice for car camping with boat.

- Four lane all tides ramps and floats
- Lots of long term fee parking ($10+ day)
- Transient floats for overnights
- Small convenience store, short walk
- Hiking trails
- Small bathroom
- You have the option of going through near by Deception Pass or using Swinomish channel to avoid weather issues.
- On shore campgrounds (not really walking distance to moorage)

## Washington Park in Anacortes

City park (campground) with ramp. **This is your #1 choice for car camping with a boat.** You can go out for day trips, and then keep the boat on the trailer at your camp site. Or splash the boat and take off for a week or more. Parking fee used to be $8 day. Calling for reservations is a must for summer camping.

- Two lane ramp, and float (sometimes part covered with sand and seaweed)
- Limited amount of fee parking, but long term is ok, or park at your camp site
- Subject to wakes
- Bathrooms (nice kybo's) with showers
- No overnight boat tie up, but you could anchor out
- On shore campground, would make good home base for day only boating or large groups where some stay in camp while others go boating.
- Just a few miles to stores in town
- Absolute closest jump off point to San Juans

## Twin Bridges

County ramp at north end of Swinomish Channel, under the bridge. (I have used once, I didn't like it)
- Two lane ramp with float
- Strong current a lot of the time
- Shallow at low tide (too shallow to use for some boats at low tide) (the main reason I didn't like it)
- Over used bathroom
- Questionable security in long term fee parking lot
- No stores, no nothing

# *Kayak Day Paddles and Camping Trips*

It is impossible to list all the ways to go kayaking in the San Juan's, but I will float a few ideas your way.

## For Kayakers Only

1. Very basic trips - Take the ferry to Friday Harbor, drive to San Juan County Park, set up camp in your reserved camp site. Beach launch your tandem and singles and paddle less than two miles down Haro Strait to Whale Watch Park hoping to get some orca photo ops. Later - car top your boats to Roche Harbor where you splash them again and take a spin around the bay stopping by one acre Posey Island. Keep up this blistering pace daily until it's time to head for home.
2. Try this same idea on Orcas Island, camping at Moran State Park, or on Lopez staying at Spencer Spit.
3. For a little more fun, consider a night or two at each island sampling the nearby waters each day.
4. For more kayak action try this – Take the ferry to Orcas, drive to Deer Harbor, Pay $10 per day to park the car. Now paddle off with all your overnight gear. Your destination is Jones Island only two miles away where you will camp in the campground just for boaters arriving in human powered craft.
5. Lets get serious. This time, take the ferry to Orcas, drive to Eastsound, stock up at Island Market. Drive five blocks to the north end of Beach Rd where you will park your rig and beach launch your boats. It's only a short 2 ½ miles to Fossil Bay on Sucia where you can have a reserved camp site waiting your arrival or paddle into one of the more remote campsites in Shallow, Snoring or Ewing coves. Sucia's myriad bays, coves and shoreline are premier protected paddling waters.

The variations are truly endless – here are some more ideas.

- Leave your car at Orcas Landing and paddle straight to Jones Island - four miles, five if you swing into Deer Harbor for lunch at the deli on the dock.
- Leave your car at Roche Harbor and paddle to Stuart Island for a night or two. It's less than five miles to the kayaker campground.
- For the budget Eco minded kayak enthusiast try this variation. Start out by leaving your car in long term parking at the Anacortes ferry terminal. Board the ferry with your gear laden kayaks (it takes two to carry two) or bring dollies. Disembark on foot at Friday Harbor or Orcas Landing on your way to Jones, or if you get off at Friday, you can launch your kayak at the dinghy dock and paddle less than two miles to Turn Island State Park. After setting up camp paddle back to Friday Harbor for a night on the town, but be sure to bring flashlight markers or make it back to camp before dark.

## Bicycle Variations

- Our family brings bicycles and kayaks on our boat and our cars. Here is what you can do when thinking outside the box. Chain your bike to the bike rack on the esplanade at Friday Harbor. Next, drive your car and kayak to Jackson Beach, lock up, launch and paddle around Turn Point and Pear Point back to the dinghy dock at Friday. Get on your bike and peddle to Jackson Beach to retrieve the car. This little exercise takes a solid ¾ day leaving you time for shopping and an early dinner before heading to your campsite for s'mores at San Juan County Park.
- One time my daughter parked her car at Washington Park in Anacortes, she then rode her bike one mile to the ferry. She got off at Orcas and pedaled to Eastsound for a lunchtime brewery tour. That afternoon she hitched a boat ride with me from the county dock at Eastsound to her reserved waterfront campsite at Odlin Park. The next two days she kayaked and biked Lopez.

**I hope I have opened a few doors and encouraged you to shine a light on what you really would like to do and see. Get creative and make the most of the San Juan Islands.**

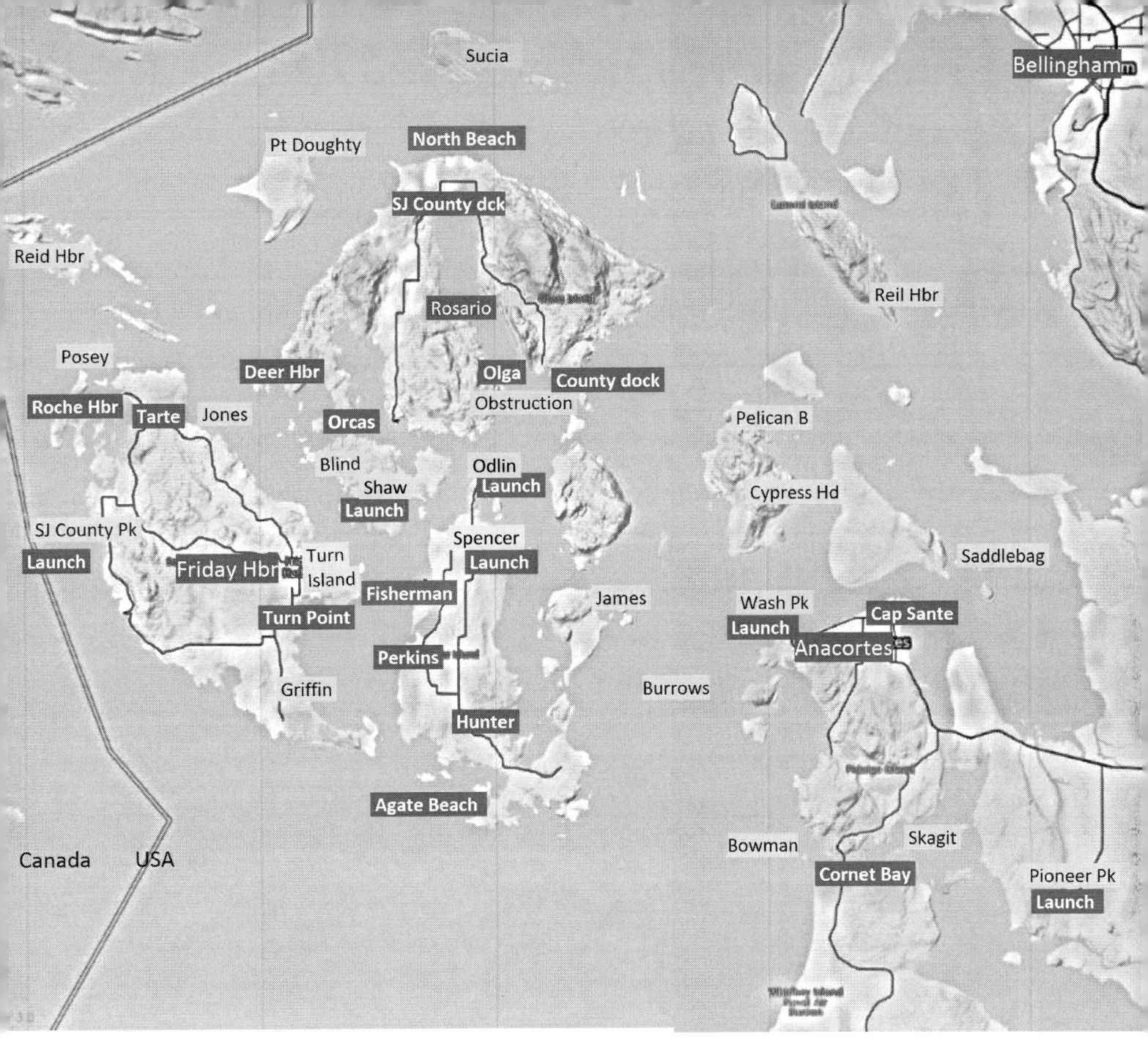

Campsites = black type — Launch points = white type

## Kayaker camp sites and launch points

Campsites designated – *human powered vessels only* – may require sharing group sites. Many of the sites are within existing fee campgrounds. At the end of the camp site list are – *launch only* – sites (white type) where overnight parking may not be allowed. Launching and parking at resorts may require permission and payment.

# Kayaker and human or wind powered campsites and launch sites, including Cascadia Marine Trail sites

SP = State Park   Fee = yes
CP = County Park Fee = yes
DNR = Dept. Nat Resources - no fee
PL = Park and Launch

Point Doughty - Orcas Island DNR
Latitude: 48.42.682
Longitude: 12256.966

Reil Hbr - Lummi Island - DNR
Latitude: 48.65875
Longitude: -122.6142

Pelican Beach - Cypress Island DNR
Latitude: 48.602
Longitude: -122.7037

Cypress Head - Cypress Island DNR
Latitude: 48.5685
Longitude: -122.6703

Saddlebag Island SP
Latitude: 48.5352
Longitude: -122.555916

Washington Park - Anacortes City Pk
latitude: 48.5005
longitude: -122.697

Burrows Island - SP
Latitude: 48.48158
Longitude: -122.68971

James Island - SP
Latitude: 48.51015
Longitude: -122.776916

Pioneer Park - La Conner City Pk PL
Latitude: 48.3862
Longitude: -122.5014

Skagit Island SP
Latitude: 48.41525
Longitude: -122.577466

Bowman Bay SP - Latitude: 48.41516
Longitude: -122.650516

Obstruction Pass - Orcas Isl. SP
Latitude: 48.601666
Longitude: -122.82785

Spencer Spit - Lopez Isl SPL
Latitude: 48.534866
Longitude: -122.857783

Odlin County Pk - Lopez Isl CP
Latitude: 48.557816
Longitude: -122.89075

Shaw County Pk - Shaw Isl CPL
Latitude: 48.564516
Longitude: -122.9343

Blind Island SP
Latitude: 48.5849
Longitude: -122.9377

Jones Island SP
Latitude: 48.616216
Longitude: -123.051966

Griffin Bay -San Juan Isl SP
Latitude: 48.4761
Longitude: -123.0101

San Juan County Pk CPL
Smallpox Bay
Latitude: 48.541766
Longitude: -123.15935

Posey Island SP
Latitude: 48.61815
Longitude: -123.167816

Reid Hbr - Stuart Isl SP
Latitude: 48.676
Longitude: -123.204

Turn Island SP
Latitude: 48.5307
Longitude: 122.9746

Sucia Island SP
Latitude: 48.7528
Longitude: 122.9050

Continued from prior page
## Kayak sites for Launching only  *"white"* type on map

**North Beach Rd** in Eastsound
Orcas Island - PL
latitude: 48.714
longitude: -122.9049333

**Fisherman Bay** Lopez Isl. PL
Kayak Shop
latitude: 48.51416667
longitude: -122.9117667

**Orcas Landing** + long term pkg
Latitude: 48.5975
Longitude: -122.9442

**San Juan County Dock** in
Eastsound
Latitude: 48.6915
Longitude: 122.9046

**Squalicum Hbr** Marina -
Bellingham
Latitude: 48.7563
Longitude: 122.4949

**Friday Hbr** Marina
Latitude: 48.5362
Longitude: 123.0154

**Cap Sante** Marina - Anacortes
Latitude: 48.5137
Longitude: -122.6094

**Deer Hbr** Marina - Orcas
Latitude: 48.6200
Longitude: 123.0013

**Turn Point** - San Juan
Latitude: 48.5256
Longitude: 122.9741

**Jackson Beach** - San Juan
Latitude: 48.5194
Longitude: 123.0130

**Roche Hbr** Resort - San Juan
Latitude: 48.6085
Longitude: 123.1524

**Rosario** Resort - Orcas
Latitude: 48.6461
Longitude: 122.8709

**Olga** community dock - Orcas
Latitude: 48.6191
Longitude: 122.8355

**SJ county dock** - End of
Obstruction Pass Rd - Orcas
Latitude: 48.6057
Longitude: 122.8165

**Cornet Bay** - Deception Pass
Latitude: 48.4025
Longitude: -122.6206

**Agate Beach** day use - Lopez
Latitude: 48.4280
Longitude: 122.8774

**Hunter Bay** Lopez - county
dock/ramp
Latitude: 48.4596
Longitude: 122.8487

**Otis Perkins** day use - Lopez
Latitude: 48.5050
Longitude: 122.9344

**English Camp** day use - San
Juan
Latitude: 48.5860
Longitude: 123.1504

**SJ County Pk** San Juan at
Smallpox Bay
Latitude: 48.5417
Longitude: -123.1593

**Reuben Tarte** day use San Juan
Latitude: 48.6122
Longitude: 123.0978

**Washington Pk** - Anacortes
Launch, dock, campground,
long term pkg
Latitude: 48.5002
Longitude: 122.6924

**Spencer Spit** SP campground,
launch, day use
Latitude: 48.5366
Longitude: 122.8591

**Odlin Pk** CP campground,
launch, day use
Latitude: 48.5566
Longitude: 122.8913

**Thinking Outside** the BOX results in outstanding trips in the San Juan's

# – John's over the top Packing List –
## for those that need to bring everything

If you are new to the San Juan's as well as not too experienced in knowing what to bring, you may find some useful advice here.

We're not going to even try to be all inclusive, just some little reminders to get you thinking about your away from home needs. Obviously, you boaters and RV owners already have many things on board.

*Please, please, please, this is just a bunch of suggestions, you don't really need all this stuff to go to the San Juans. Some of the best trips (and most memorable) are minimalist – you know, "kiss" (keep it simple, stupid) Some of this list is for boaters, some for RV'rs and some for kayakers and tent campers.*

Here goes,

- I'll bet you don't have an underwater flashlight, they are great for attracting sea creatures after dark, and will add hours of entertainment time to answer your children's "I'm bored" comments. (hint, stick a cheap led flashlight in a ziplock bag) Now tie it to the end of your (floating) boat hook and poke it under water.

- How about heavy duty zip lock bags, or the ones they sell at the outdoor outfitter stores for river running, you know for your cell phone, ipod, camera, wallet, etc, etc, etc.....

- Speaking of waterproof have you got any good wood matches in a waterproof container?

- Matches mean campfires, that means you need a folding pruning saw (get a good nasty sharp one). Tip: Leave the ax, machetes, and hatchets at home because, #1 they don't work well for gathering firewood, #2 someone may get hurt and your a long way from an ER. All we use is a little razor sharp folding saw!

- Here's one you really miss and then its too late - chap-stick with spf 99 (how high do the #'s go?)

- Remember that hat that blew off into the water? ditto for glasses! you need a chin strap or leash.

- OK, this is good one, get a second or third corkscrew, uh huh! (try em at home first to make sure you can trust-em at dinner time)

- Dramamine in all forms for everyone.

- Cheap little led flashlights, lots of em, they're cheap.

- Plastic kites (not paper) for beach fun, don't forget the string.

- Multi-function tool that you carry in your pocket all the time.

- Boat, tent and RV cleaning supplies, wax, polish, paint thinner to remove tars you track on board with your shoes. We seem to do our heavy cleaning while on a cruise, I see others doing the same. Misc. boat repair supplies and tools. (sail tape, soft scrub)

Tip: Copy this list and add to it while making plans. Keep a copy on your computer and update it as needed:


**Checklist and Things to do at home before you leave, and on the day you leave:**

- create a trip planner/outline "This could be a to-do list") add to it and edit often
- pay the bills
- turn off water heater
- turn down/off furnace
- cancel paper and stop routine deliveries (have the mail held at post office)
- tell the neighbor so they can watch your house for problems
- leave a list (itinerary) and keys (with friend, relative) explaining where you are going
- leave extra keys with someone (you may need them mailed to you)

- emergency numbers (bring list, include all numbers, e-mails too)
- mow the lawn, arrange for sprinkler system operation or shut it down preferred
- arrange for pet and plant care
- make the house look lived in
- lock windows, doors, garage
- set the alarm
- set voice message
- forward calls
- turn off water
- deal with garbage service
- enable, disable computers, electronics
- unplug TV's and anything that uses a remote control or standby power
- credit/debit card info and what to do if stolen
- if your bringing a lap top, what about photo software, updates, make sure wifi works, charger, 12v inverter?

## Vehicle checks before you go

- Tip: The number one most important vehicle check is to grease your trailer bearings or possibly abort you entire cruise somewhere on the highway.
- Oil check, carry spare oil
- Tire pressure/condition (buy new tires for peace of mind)
- Spare tire and jack
- Check brake lining, master cylinder fluid
- Check hoses and carry spare coolant, atf.
- Check the belts, bring extra serpentine belt if you're traveling to or from a remote area.
- Tune up and service
- Wipers and washer fluid

- Battery check & connections, jumper cables
- Cell phone travel charger
- Do you know where and how to check fuses? (spares)
- Do you have a fire extinguisher? (Car and boat)

*Shall we dispense with all the formal bullets, they just take up a lot of space., And we have much more to cover.*

## More treasures to consider

**First aid kit,** plus prescriptions, etc: antibiotic/alcohol wipes (sealed), antiseptic cream, aspirin, motion sickness pills, bandages, burn ointment, elastic wrap, eye wash, hydrogen peroxide, Ibuprofen, insect repellent, sterile tape, scissors, snake bite kit, sterile gauze and pads, sun screen lotion, tweezers, Benadryl

**Clothing:**

Regular day wear, out on the town wear, shirts, t-shirts, trousers, jeans, dresses, sweater, raincoat, wind breaker, pajamas, swim wear, shorts, socks, joggers, hikers, sandals

**Toiletries:**

Brush, comb, toothbrush, toothpaste, floss, TP, soaps, shaving, sunscreen, deodorant, mirror, foot powder, scissors,

**Children's clothing, toiletries:** It's easy to concentrate so much on the kids you forget your own needs

**Pets, needs, etc.** (did you forget?) BTW dogs and cats are welcome, and many enjoy cruising, but we know of some dogs that get seasick. There are no parks where leash laws don't apply. Be sure to bring appropriate pfd's for pets.

Messy Tip: for boaters, consider bringing a piece of real sod (grass) for picky finicky pets – lay it on astro turf and wrap everything in a garbage bag to contain the dirt. It is cruel to subject your house trained pet to unsuitable boat conditions.

**More items to help jog the old bean, plus some good things to bring along but often forgot.**

Aluminum foil, camp cook kit, cooking oil, corkscrew, cutting board, flatware, spices, knife, measure cup, paper towels, plastic cups, trash bags, pot holder, tongs, spatula, matches, zip lock bags, flashlight, batteries, travel alarm, cell phone, gps, map, rain poncho, chocolate, pet needs! CASH, camera and tripod, medicines, hard copy of friends and relatives phone numbers in case your cell phone quits. weather report, books, sunglasses, binoculars, contact lens

You can pick up what you forget along the way.

prep. hats, laundry/wash bags, mini sewing kit, playing cards and games, car inverter to run chargers.

This list is not all inclusive and needs your additions/subtractions as you prepare for your travels. (Take a deep breath now) More to come.

**Important numbers & things**

Passwords for getting online and atm banking etc.

do not rely on cell phone or laptop memory for numbers/names/addresses (make a hard copy)

auto insurance info. Your automobile license number (in case its stolen)

do you have current hard pictures of everyone?

serious medical condition information

passports, photo ID, vaccination proof, reservations, birth certificates

**Had enough of lists ?**

Don't toss in the towel just yet, but it is time to lighten up. This preparation exercise is really a one time thing that never gets completely finished. As you travel again and again, you will simply add to your arsenal. Usually when you realize you forgot something like marshmallow & hot dog sticks, you improvise. Aha, now use your pocket multi tool and cut some sticks (crisis averted).

Remember that minimalist comment at the beginning of this list, it may have some merit. – Kiss

**Tip:** One of the first things to learn about packing is that you can't bring everything, and that everything you bring must fit somewhere. The problem with packing boats and RV's is that when you begin using stuff, everything expands, and you are forced to wallow in the mess.

It pays to consolidate at home, avoid unnecessary packaging, plan meals and snacks that don't generate trash. Avoid bringing cases and cases of drinks and other plastics. Have a plan for containing trash and on longer boat outings arrange to visit marina dumpsters.

## Urgent care - Emergency

San Juan County Sheriff - 96 2nd St, Friday Harbor WA

(360) 378-4151   **emergency - 911**

**Anacortes:**
Island Hospital
1211 24th St, Anacortes, WA 98221
Phone: (360) 299-1300

**Orcas Island:** Orcas medical center
7 Deye Lane (PO Box 1269), Eastsound,
WA 98245 - 360-376-2561
(Next to Orcas Center on Mt. Baker Road)

**Lopez Island** Medical Clinic (in the village)
103 Washburn Pl, Lopez Island, WA 98261
Phone:(360) 468-2245

**San Juan Island:**
Peace Health Peace Island Medical
Center 1117 Spring Street
Friday Harbor, WA 98250
360-378-2141

### Kayak and Bicycle rental and repair

**Lopez Island** Sea Kayak
& Lopez Bicycle Works
2847 Fisherman Bay Rd
(360) 468 2847

**Orcas Island**
Wildlife Cycles
350 N Beach Rd
Eastsound - (360-376-4708

Outer Island Expeditions
Eastsound - (360) 376-3711

**San Juan Island**
Island Bicycles - 380 Argyle Av
Friday Harbor (360) 378 4941

Outer Island Expeditions
Roche Harbor - 360 378 5767

It is impossible for me to personally know the clinics and rental shops listed, so I won't review any. However, I want to give you some phone numbers and addresses on each island to at least get you pointed in the right direction if you need some help. These numbers were good in 2016

# Resources every boater in the San Juan's needs to know

New boaters are tech savvy and may not have learned (the hard way) why old salts are called old salts. Electronics quit, signals fade, batteries fry, and complex instructions are less than useless when trouble strikes.

**I recommend every boater to the San Juans obtain these time tested aids**

1. Current Atlas (Canadian Hydrographic service) search Amazon books for **"Juan de Fuca Current Atlas"** You will need to purchase the Current Atlas and the annual companion index.
2. Print a local tide forecast for your travel dates.
**https://tidesandcurrents.noaa.gov/noaatidepredictions/NOAATidesFacade.jsp?Stationid=9449880**
3. Print or at least review the Noaa weather and sea forecast -
**http://marine.weather.gov/MapClick.php?lat=48.49385744305437&lon=-122.75436401367188#.WCs2oy0rKUk**
4. Noaa charts -
**http://www.charts.noaa.gov/OnLineViewer/18421.shtml**

Chart 18421 is a overview of the entire area - in addition you may want some larger scale charts that cover smaller areas, but this is the one I use. It conveniently folds in quarters and fits in my acrylic protective cover. Of course I use my techie chart plotter also.

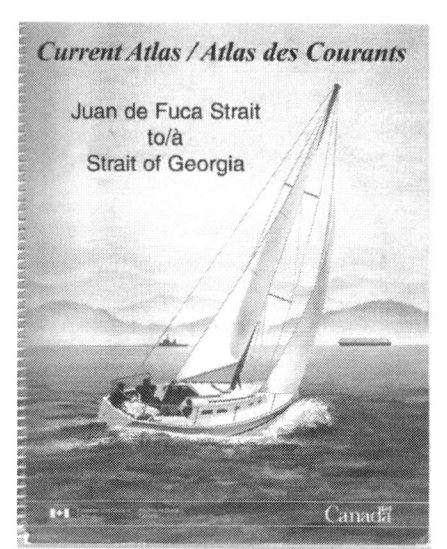

*Words of Wisdom*
*Chosen to make you think*

- Can everyone run the boat? Anyone other than you? - only you?

- You can save a man overboard - Yes? - How? – Who can save you, **yes you?** - really? - How?

- How will you plug a big puncture hole? – ok, a big crack? – seriously, you have two minutes!

- Does everyone know how to use the radio to call for help and is the information written down?

- Do you have required day and night rescue signals?

- Washington requires you to have the mandatory boater education card for your state.

- Can your insurance pay for anything you hit or are responsible for?

- Can all your crew tie a bowline knot? - Can you tie one behind your back? - One handed?

# Authors Note – from me to you
### *This is a **Land and Sea Guidebook to** the San Juans*

*T*hanks for using my book, I really mean it! First, a little about how it came about.

Long long ago, I dragged my family sailboat, little kids and wife to Olympia WA where we launched at Swantown Marina. The five of us were going to the San Juan's, and Victoria. I thought that's how you did it. In retrospect, my plan needed help, but we had fun and have been coming back ever since. I remember back then, how the information available, while quite detailed, wasn't much use to us. — What I really needed to know was where to park the car, get gas on the water, and locate bathrooms little children would use.

Fast forward to 2014 — the kids are grown and leading their own forays' to the Islands. I have ridden all the ferries with and without a car, hiked, biked, camped and boated to my heart's content. I suspected many of you were experiencing the same frustrations I felt long ago, so I wrote and created my first travel book *"San Juan Islands Cruise Guide"* a guidebook specifically for boaters facing what we had conquered.

Jump to 2017 – I decided to create my second travel book. A book that left the water and focused on land bound travel, but it was impossible to ignore all the islands that are accessible only by water. The result is a combination guide for car travelers arriving by ferry intent on staying on dry land but not ignoring boaters either.

This guidebook is my attempt to share what I have learned along the way, not just a library list of places, and parks, but useful information I know will help you have a great time. I have tried to fill in the local knowledge gaps and answer the not so silly questions while avoiding dated, useless, flowery descriptions.

The book is for all visitors to the San Juan Islands, and very importantly, I have included notes and tips about nearby cities, parks, marinas and resort facilities to enhance and make your San Juan travels a resounding success.

# Index

## A
Afterglow Mausoleum......... 53
Agate Beach County Park.. 136
Alpaca............................ 40
American Camp................. 37
Anacortes...................... 117
anchoring............... 21, 33, 43
aquarium......................... 26

## B
Bellingham................. 20-22
biking............................ 18
Blakely's...................... 122
Boat fuel...................... 152
Boat ramp...................... 21
boaters and kayakers........ 127
Boundary Pass Traders....... 71
Bowman Bay.................. 110
breakwater................ 26, 28
Butchart Gardens 10, 13, 143, 144, 146, 147

## C
Cap Sante....................... 22
Cap Sante Marina...... 117, 119
Cattle Pass.... 33, 35-37, 41, 42
Cattle Point................ 37-39
Cattle Point Lighthouse....... 24
Clark Island State Park........ 97
Cornet Bay 21-22, 109, 110, 112-116, 119
Customs and Canada........ 150
Cypress Island................ 103
Cypress Head............ 103, 104

## D
Deception Pass........ 10, 21, 22
Deception Pass Tours........ 114
Deer Harbor Resort.. 74, 81-83
Department of Natural Resources.................. 103

Doe Island State Park.......... 96
Dog Park......... 27, 30, 85, 118

## E
Eagle Bluff hike................. 104
Eagle Cove Beach............... 39
Eagle Harbor............ 103-104
Eastsound....................... 13
Eastsound County Dock...... 86
Eastsound Dog Park........... 85
Echo Bay................... 22, 100
Eddie & Friends Dog Park.... 27
emergency................ 161, 163
English Camp 31, 37, 38, 40-43
Ewing Cove....................... 98

## F
Fairground....................... 32
ferries.. 12 - 15, 17-20, 26, 165
Fisherman Bay.................. 12
flag ceremony.................... 59
Fort Whitman.................. 115
Fossil Bay................... 98, 100
Fourth of July Beach........... 38
Fourth of July fireworks...... 28
Fox Cove......................... 98
Friday Harbor 12, 13, 17-19, 23, 26, 28, 31-34, 37, 38
Friday Harbor Marina Map. 29
fuel.......................... 26, 28
Fuel and Grocery Stores on the Water..................... 152

## G
Garrison Bay................ 41-43
Goat Island.................... 115

## H
Haro Strait......... 37, 39, 41, 42
Hazard warning 78, 95, 97, 101, 102, 107, 113
Hope Island.................... 115
Hotel De Haro.................. 60
Hummel Lake.................. 134

Hunter Bay County Dock and boat ramp...................... 137

## I
Iceberg point.................. 136
Inati Bay....................... 102
interpretive center.. 38, 41, 42
Islands Marine Center....... 139

## J
Jackles Lagoon................... 38
Jackson Beach Park............. 36
James Island Marine Park. 121
Jones Island...................... 74
Juan De Fuca............... 22, 36
Judd Bay.......................... 86

## K
Kayak Day Paddles............ 156
Kayak tip.............. 75, 97, 81
kayakers.................... 19, 33
Kayaking small boats from Roche Harbor..................... 73
Kings Market.............. 26, 28
Krystal Acres Alpaca Farm... 40

## L
La Conner... 10, 14-15, 21, 107
Lafarge Open Space....... 35-36
Lakedale Resort................. 31
Lakedale Resort at Three Lakes............................... 65
Launching Ramps............. 154
Lime Kiln.................... 31, 40
Lime Kiln Point State Park... 47
Lopez Farm Cottages......... 133
Lopez Island................ 12, 123
Lopez Islander Resort Marina 140
Lopez Village 12, 123, 126-127

## M

Mackaye Harbor Boat Launch............ 137
Maiden of Deception Pass................ 111
Matia Island State Park.... 97
Mausoleum.................... 53
Moran State Park............ 13
Mosquito Pass................ 43
Mt. Constitution.............. 13

## O

Obstruction Pass State Park.............. 94
Odlin County Park.......... 128
Olga............................... 93
orca.................... 27, 45, 46
Orcas Island................... 13
Orcas Island Map............ 79
Orcas Landing................. 81
Otis Perkins Day Park..... 138
Outer Islands.................. 13

## P

Packing List.................... 160
Patos Island .....................101
Pelican Beach.......... 103-104
Pelindaba Lavender Farm  40
Pickett's Monument........ 38
Pig War................. 37, 41, 42
Prevost Harbor........... 67, 69

## R

ramp.......... 14, 18, 20-22, 36
Red Fox........................... 38
Reid Harbor................ 67, 69
Reid Harbor float............ 70
Roche Harbor 28, 31, 36, 41-43
Roche Harbor area map... 44
Roche Harbor history....... 56
Roche Harbor Map........... 64
Rosario Beach................ 111
Rosario Resort................ 88
Rueben Tarte Memorial Park ........................................ 66

RV's................................ 19

## S

Saddlebag Island................ 106
sailboat........................ 22, 165
Salish................................ 10
salt water aquarium.............. 26
San Juan County Park........... 45
San Juan Island 1, 3, 10, 12-13, 23, 25, 31, 33, 36-37, 42, 165
San Juan Island  – Quick Check 24
San Juan Island Transit.......... 31
San Juan Vineyard................ 31
Saturday Farmers Market..... 26
Sculpture Park...................... 31
Shallow Bay.......................... 98
Shark Reef Sanctuary.......... 135
Sharpe Cove........ 109, 110, 111
Shaw Island....... 12, 17, 18, 141
SJ County Park........... 31, 45-46
Skagit County........................ 21
Skagit Island....................... 115
slip assignment.................... 28
Smallpox Bay................... 45-46
Snoring Cove........................ 98
Snug Harbor Resort............... 31
Southend General Store and Restaurant......................... 137
Spencer Spit State Park....... 131
Squalicum Harbor...... 10, 20-22
Stuart Island.................... 67-70
Stuart Island County Dock..... 73
Sucia Island State Park.......... 98
Swinomish Channel 21, 106, 107

## T

tent camping........................ 32
Tips.... 10, 16, 20, 21, 26, 28, 31, 33, 35, 37, 45, 60, 68,  93, 98, 100, 102,  104, 117, 120
Trail to Turn Point Lighthouse 70
transit............................ 31, 42
Turn Island.................... 33-34
Turn Point..................... 33, 35

Turn Point Lighthouse........... 68
Turtleback Mountain............ 82
Twin Bridges.................. 21, 22

## U

Urgent care - Emergency.... 163

## V

Vancouver........................... 148
Victoria............................ 10, 26

## W

Washington Park 21, 78, 97, 119
West Beach Resort Marina... 87
West Sound.......................... 81
Whale Museum..................... 27
Whale Watch Park..... 31, 46, 47

167

# Mileage Chart

| Rosario ………. ROS | Saddlebag Is ….. SDL | James Is …………. JMS |
|---|---|---|
| Roche Hbr …….. RH | Deer Harbor ……DRH | Jones Is …………. JOS |
| Sucia …………….. SUC | Orcas Landing … ORC | Fisherman Bay … FSB |
| La Conner ……. LAC | Cap Sante ……… CAP | Cornet Bay ……… COR |
| Squalicum Hbr SQU | Pelican Beach ….. PB | Inati Bay ……….. INB |
| Stuart Is …………. STU | Blakely's …………. BLK | Smallpox Bay ….. SPB |
| | | Friday Hbr……….. FRY |

The distances are *water miles* pulled off a chart plotter and are estimates following the shortest route while staying on the inside of the islands where practical. Kayakers must be careful not to exceed their abilities or under estimate the effect of currents and wind.

|     | ROS | JOS | RH | SUC | LAC | SPB | IINB | SQU | STU | SDL | DRH | ORC | CAP | PB | BLK | JMS | FSB | COR | FRY |
|-----|-----|-----|----|-----|-----|-----|------|-----|-----|-----|-----|-----|-----|----|-----|-----|-----|-----|-----|
| ROS |     | 11  | 16 | 18  | 25.5| 20  | 15   | 21  | 17.5| 16  | 10  | 6   | 17  | 8  | 4   | 9   | 8.5 | 19  | 10.5|
| JOS | 11  |     | 5  | 10  | 29.5| 10  | 20   | 27.5| 6.5 | 22  | 2.5 | 5   | 21.5| 14.5| 9.5| 13.5| 8.5 | 23.5| 6   |
| RH  | 16  | 5   |    | 14.5| 34  | 5   | 25   | 32  | 4   | 27  | 7.5 | 10  | 26  | 19 | 14.5| 18  | 12.5| 29  | 10  |
| SUC | 18  | 10  | 14.5|    | 27  | 18  | 13   | 19  | 12.5| 16.5| 12  | 15  | 21  | 12.5| 15 | 17  | 21  | 21  | 16.5|
| LAC | 25.5| 29.5| 34 | 27  |     | 32  | 18   | 23  | 36  | 9   | 28  | 24  | 9.5 | 16 | 19.5| 16.5| 26.5| 9   | 27.5|
| SPB | 20  | 10  | 5  | 18  | 32  |     | 30   | 36  | 15  | 31  | 12  | 14  | 12  | 24 | 19  | 22  | 20  | 25  | 14  |
| INB | 15  | 20  | 25 | 13  | 18  | 30  |      | 7   | 26  | 8.5 | 19  | 16  | 11  | 7  | 11  | 12.5| 16  | 25  | 18  |
| SQU | 21  | 27.5| 32 | 19  | 23  | 36  | 7    |     | 31  | 14  | 25  | 22  | 16  | 13 | 17.5| 19  | 24  | 25  | 26.5|
| STU | 17.5| 6.5 | 4  | 12.5| 36  | 15  | 26   | 31  |     | 28.5| 9   | 11  | 21  | 21 | 16  | 19  | 14  | 29  | 11.5|
| SDL | 16  | 22  | 27 | 16.5| 9   | 31  | 8.5  | 14  | 28.5|     | 20.5| 17  | 2.5 | 7.5| 12.5| 9.5 | 18.5| 17.5| 21  |
| DRH | 10  | 2.5 | 7.5| 12  | 28  | 12  | 19   | 25  | 9   | 20.5|     | 4   | 19  | 13 | 8   | 11.5| 8   | 21  | 5.5 |
| ORC | 6   | 5   | 10 | 15  | 24  | 14  | 16   | 22  | 11  | 15.5| 4   |     | 16  | 9  | 4.5 | 8   | 5   | 18  | 7   |
| CAP | 17  | 21.5| 26 | 21  | 9.5 | 12  | 11   | 16  | 21  | 2.5 | 19  | 16  |     | 8.5| 11  | 8.5 | 17  | 13  | 19.5|
| PB  | 8   | 14  | 19 | 14.5| 16  | 24  | 7    | 13  | 21  | 7.5 | 13  | 9   | 8.5 |    | 4.5 | 8   | 11  | 15  | 13.5|
| BLK | 4   | 9.5 | 14.5| 15 | 19.5| 19  | 11   | 17.5| 16  | 12.5| 8   | 5   | 11  | 4.5|     | 5.5 | 6.5 | 15  | 8.5 |
| JMS | 9   | 13.5| 18 | 17  | 16.5| 22  | 12.5 | 19  | 19  | 9.5 | 11.5| 8   | 8.5 | 8  | 5.5 |     | 9.5 | 9.5 | 12  |
| FSB | 8.5 | 8.5 | 12.5| 21 | 26.5| 20  | 16   | 24  | 14  | 18.5| 8   | 5   | 17  | 11 | 6.5 | 9.5 |     | 19.5| 4   |
| COR | 19  | 23.5| 29 | 21  | 9   | 25  | 25   | 25  | 29  | 17.5| 21  | 18  | 13  | 15 | 15  | 9.5 | 19.5|     | 22  |
| FRY | 10.5| 6   | 10 | 16.5| 27.5| 14  | 18   | 26.5| 11.5| 21  | 5.5 | 7   | 19.5| 13.5| 8.5| 12  | 4   | 22  |     |